# MATH-O-GRAPHS
## Critical Thinking Through Graphing

Donna Kay Buck
and
Francis H. Hildebrand

© 1990

Midwest Publications • Critical Thinking Press & Software
P.O. Box 448
Pacific Grove, CA   93950

ISBN  0-89455-421-2

# ABOUT THE AUTHORS

## DONNA KAY BUCK

Ms. Buck holds a Masters Degree in Mathematics from Western Washington University. She has had 23 years of classroom teaching experience, at all grade levels, and has taught math and science abroad at the American Schools in Pakistan, Brazil, Tunisia, Liberia, and Morocco.

She currently serves as a mathematics specialist for gifted children in the Port Angeles School District in the state of Washington. Mrs. Buck conducts inservice training workshops in the teaching of thinking skills, in means of integrating mathematics and science in the classroom, and in mathematics instruction through use of concrete manipulatives. She has also been a featured speaker at numerous conferences and universities across the nation and has presented national and regional workshops for the National Council of the Teachers of Mathematics and for various associations for gifted students.

## FRANCIS H. HILDEBRAND

Francis Hildebrand received his Ph. D. in Mathematics Education from Michigan State University. He has taught mathematics for the Extended Learning Program of Central Michigan University and currently teaches mathematics and mathematics education at Western Washington University.

His 33 years of classroom experience spans all grades from kindergarten through college. He continues to conduct inservice training across the United States, including Alaska, Hawaii, and the Pacific Islands.

# ACKNOWLEDGEMENTS

Many people have contributed indirectly to the kinds of problems presented in this book. Individuals include Professor Lois Redmond of Central Michigan University, Professor Gail Adele of the University of Idaho, Professor Cal Collier (Ret.) of Michigan State University, and Patty Mitchell and Sharon Bettis of Western Washington University, as well as public school teachers Shannon Woodward, Amy Hughes, Peggy Johnson, Peter Anderson, Beth Burns, Diane Chase, and Lisa Mennard. Dr. Jayasri Ghosh-Manior, Mel Chopp, and John Rosmaryn, all formerly of the Tacoma Public Schools, contributed greatly to the concepts presented here.

Marilyn Burns, who teaches a wonderful math solutions course, and Lyle Fisher, who generates such challenging problems, served as sources of inspiration.

Additional thanks goes to groups of teachers from inservice sections spanning many years, including the school districts of Anchorage Borough (Alaska), Hilo (Hawaii), and more than twenty districts from the state of Michigan.

Finally, but far from least, is our editor, Carole Bannes, who made many improvements in both layout and wording, and our spouses, James G. Buck and Margaret Cochrane (Hildebrand), who have edited, listened, and tolerated our preoccupation.

~ ~ *Donna Kay Buck*
~ ~ *Francis H. Hildebrand*

# TABLE OF CONTENTS

# INTRODUCTION TO MATH-O-GRAPHS

## Objective: Critical Thinking in the Classroom

MATH-O-GRAPHS activities are structured to provide a means of inviting critical thinking into your classroom. Each activity proceeds through several steps:

- begins with objectives that meet the NCTM standards;
- presents an initial graph for anticipatory discussion and vocabulary development questions;
- moves into creating a class graph for processing information;
- develops mathematical and graphic strategies for solving a math problem; and
- concludes by offering extending activities for reinforcing mathematical concepts through further exploration, strategy development, and analysis and evaluation of the problem (or similar preceeding problems).

The initial graph is intended to be used before the main problem is presented to the class. It may be projected from an overhead onto the chalkboard or drawn on butcher paper so students can record their individual responses. The initial graph allows students an opportunity for covert thinking and independent problem solving.

Class graphs involve joining others in a cooperative exploration and exchange of views on possible strategies to solve the problem. Teachers may wish to concentrate on the initial graph one day and introduce the problem the next.

Both the graphs and the discussion questions can be used to stress the relevance of mathematics to the real world and to past knowledge and experiences students may have had. Verbalization of student problem-solving processes are encouraged; nonverbal awareness is helped to consciousness.

As students develop and use graphs, they visualize, recognize, create, and extend patterns as they make connections among the various components of math problems.

## The Role of the Student

MATH-O-GRAPHS activities ask students to coordinate many types of thinking, not just problem solving or computation, as they attack imaginative, real-world problems.

- Students will use various analysis processes as they organize and synthesize data to hypothesize or create possible solutions. (A detailed Teacher's Guide page opposite each activity will help teachers demonstrate strategies and facilitate students through the use of facts and concepts at higher reasoning levels. Students will develop new insights into their own analysis procedures and develop abilities for critical reflection.)
- Students will recognize that a given problem may have several solutions, each of which should be evaluated so the less practical ones can be discarded. Strategies for arriving at possible solutions must be stressed because the correct solution is second in importance to the thinking processes used to get there.
- Students will use deductive and inductive thinking as they test possible solutions for extension into unknown cases. The extensions are large enough (and open-ended enough) to encompass real-world problems so that evaluation and application of concepts can take place.
- Students will learn to associate and integrate information from other students with their own knowledge. Extensive class-discussion questions relate each activity topic to mathematics and to other curriculum areas.

All of these individual processes are part of the larger process of critical thinking. In mathematics, this means that teachers must encourage students to break away from the usual, rule-oriented learning style, to develop and apply their own successful strategies, and to become open to alternative strategies and solutions suggested by others.

## The Role of the Teacher

It is important to note that all innovative teachers, not just mathematics teachers, use and like the MATH-O-GRAPHS activities. All teachers who sees problem solving and thinking skills as essential will enjoy exploring these problems with their students.

All activities in this book have been field tested by at least six classes at various schools and have been found suitable for grades 4–8. The non-grade identifiable, easy-to-follow format enables teachers to use the book based on skill, rather than grade, level.

Activities are organized into generalized-topic units that complement most typical classroom math texts. However, since the problems address many skills in math, they may be used as a supplementary learning aid without relating them to any specific text.

## The Role of Class Discussion

Teachers can encourage solid learning by providing a classroom environment that encourages open discussion, a free exchange of ideas, and an exploration of thinking strategies that lead to answers—incorrect as well as correct ones. This enables students to evaluate their own reasoning and, if necessary, to substitute different approaches or methods that work better.

Teachers should help students compare and define variables, develop and strengthen vocabulary necessary for comprehending the problem, and distinguish relevant from irrelevant information. (See page 1 of the text for a list of possible questions for stimulating class discussion.)

By guiding class discussion, teachers will strengthen students' thinking concepts, as well as gather immediate feedback on student progress (thus cutting down or eliminating the need to grade paperwork).

## Rationale

Teachers in all disciplines have been highly impressed with the way MATH-O-GRAPHS activities help students transfer their thinking skills and apply them to problems encountered in daily life. Activities in this book focus on encouraging students to use multiple approaches as they search for fresh insights, alternative strategies, and workable solutions to any problem situation.

MATH-O-GRAPHS stresses the elements of good thinking as a mathematical tool to be used toward understanding concepts and attacking problems. Most of us have had the experience of cramming for tests—only to promptly forget much of the information once the tests were over (if not before). This manner of education was, to some extent, the result of a system that emphasized rote recall and a single answer. In mathematics this meant drilling on computation algorithms.

Now, however, the emphasis is changing. Educators are focusing on the importance of critical thinking in all disciplines and the advantages such thinking methods give to those students who learn to apply them. As a result, many educators are preparing lessons that focus on teaching students how to analyze, develop, and utilize their thinking processes. The primary goal of this book is to help the classroom teacher in this pursuit.

# SUGGESTED QUESTIONS FOR CLASS DISCUSSION

*These questions are intended to serve as suggestions or guides for areas or topics that might be discussed as the class considers a graph. All questions, needless to say, cannot be applied to all graphs. Neither is this meant to be a complete listing. Please add, delete, or edit as you and your students see fit.*

- What can you tell from looking at this graph?
- Which area of the graph shows the greatest (or least) response? Do you think that would always be true?
- Are there areas of the graph which show equal responses? What does this indicate?
- Does anything about the results shown on this graph surprise you?
- Is it possible that an individual's mark would not fit on the graph? If so, where would it be placed?
- Could you mark more than one spot on this graph? Why would you want to?
- Would you expect this graph to show different responses if used in South America, Europe, Asia, Africa, or Australia?
- Would you expect this graph to have different responses if used with different age groups?
- How might this graph change when used in a city (or a farming area)?
- What could you do with this information? What type of profession or job might be able to use this information? How would they use it?
- How might the information be used as part of an advertisement?
- If you could add one more part to this graph, what would it be?
- Why does the design of this graph work better than another?
- Write a brief summary of the information concluded from this graph. Can you use the information in the graph to create a story or a poem? A newspaper article?

# DOUBLE THE DIGIT

**Initial Graph...**
Choose one city listed below. Mark the diagram based on the year that city was founded.

| City | Founding Date |
|------|------|
| Chicago | 1803 |
| Hong Kong | 1842 |
| Leningrad | 1703 |
| New York | 1624 |
| San Juan | 1521 |

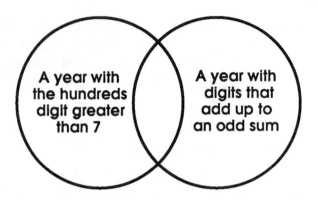

**Speaking of Dates...**
- Which cities listed above have founding dates that would be outside the diagram? Which would be in the intersection?
- Do you know the founding date of the city you live in (or near)? If so, where would it go on the diagram? If you don't know when this city was founded, how could you find out?

**Focus Question...**
- Which cities on the chart have a hundreds digit greater than 7 in their founding date? Which have a tens digit greater than the hundreds digit? Which place digit do all the founding dates above have in common?
- Which founding dates have an odd-digit sum? Are the digit sums of any of the founding dates equal?

**Problem...**
Ariel and Erwin live in the town of Sweethome. It was founded in a special year, for in that year:
- the tens digit was twice the units digit
- the hundreds digits was twice the tens digit
- the thousands digit was less than any of the other digits
- the sum of the digits of that year was 15

Can you find out what year Sweethome was founded? Can you use a graph to justify your answer?

# DOUBLE THE DIGIT

### Objectives
- to develop number sense for whole numbers
- to use computation, estimation, and proportions to solve problems
- to verify and interpret results with respect to the original problem situation

### Graphing
Students can justify their answer by using a bar graph of digits by place value to illustrate comparative values of the digits.

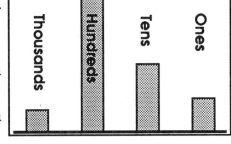

### Mathing
Some students may begin at the last statement—the sum of the digits with a total of 15. Four place values are indicated and each must be different from the others. With no regard to order, four different digits with a sum of 15 include:

| | | | |
|---|---|---|---|
| 0, 1, 5, 9 | 1, 2, 4, 8 | 1, 3, 5, 6 | 0, 1, 6, 8 |
| 1, 2, 5, 7 | 2, 3, 4, 6 | 1, 2, 3, 9 | 1, 3, 4, 7 |

The fact that one digit is twice another digit narrows the list to three possibilities:

$$1, 2, 4, 8 \qquad 2, 3, 4, 6 \qquad 1, 3, 5, 6$$

Adding the fact that another digit must be twice the second digit mentioned above narrows the choice to one:

$$1, 2, 4, 8.$$

Proper place-value positioning then results in the answer.

A second approach to this problem might begin with the information about the units digit and proceed using deductive reasoning. Zero is impossible, since the thousands digit must be less. One is impossible for the units digit, as that would leave the thousands digit as zero. Therefore, two is the smallest value possible in the units place. The tens place would then be double, or four, and the hundreds digit would be twice that, or eight. The thousands digit would be less than two and, since zero is impossible for the initial digit, one would be its value. No other value could be placed initially in the units place, since doubling that value twice would result in a hundreds digit greater than nine.

### Discussing
*"What does 'double' mean? Can it mean different things? What comes in doubles that is easy to measure? Double each of the digits in your answer and compare them. Can you find three ways to graphically demonstrate the idea of doubles?"*

### Answering
Sweethome was founded in 1842.

### Extending
- Find a year in which the tens digit is one less than the units digit, the hundreds digit three times the units digit, and the thousands digit one less than the tens digit.
- Form a problem involving the digits of the founding date of a city of your choice.

# REVERSING DIGITS

**Initial Graph...**
"Palindromes" are words that read the same backward or forward. Add another word to the verbal palindromes in the illustration.

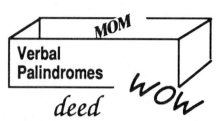

**Speaking of Palindromes...**

- How short can a verbal palindrome be? Can you think of a long one? How many letters are in the longest one you can think of? Where could you look to try to find some more?

- If you place a mirror in the middle of a palindrome, would it read the same? Why or why not?

- What would a palindrome of numbers look like? Do any of you have a house or box number that is a palindrome? A phone number?

- Are numerical palindromes easy to memorize? For example, if I quickly said a ten-digit palindrome, could you repeat it? Would it be easier to remember than another ten-digit number? Why or why not?

**Focus Question...**

- Think of a numerical palindrome with three digits. What about four digits? Five digits? Six digits?

**Problem...**
Sanford has been thinking about palindromes. **Numerical palindromes** are numbers like 22 which, when the digits are reversed, still show the same number. He is trying to think of the last time that the numbers in a year made a palindrome.

Can you help by finding that number and marking it on the number line?

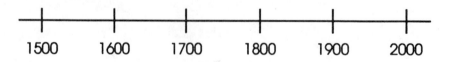

# REVERSING DIGITS

## Objectives
- to represent numerical relationships in one- and two-dimensional graphs
- to systematically collect, organize, and describe data

## Graphing
Students should be encouraged to explain how they determined where to place their mark on the given number line. To extend the graphing element further, see the **Extending** activities.

## Discussing
*"How many different dates can you think of—past or present—that can be reversed? Are any of these dates also 'mirror images'? What is the next year with a palindromic number? What about the next after that one? Where might numerical palindromes be used in the business world?"*

## Answering
The last year that the numbers actually reversed was 1881 (which was also a "mirror image" year). The next year with a palindromic number will be 1991, then 2002 (neither of which are dates with "mirror images").

## Extending
- List all the years in the first two centuries A.D. that are palindromic numbers. What pattern do you see?

| —  | 101 | 202 | 303 | 404 | 505 | 606 | 707 | 808 | 909 | 1001 |
|----|-----|-----|-----|-----|-----|-----|-----|-----|-----|------|
| 11 | 111 | 212 | 313 | 414 | 515 | 616 | 717 | 818 | 919 | 1111 |
| 22 | 121 | 222 | 323 | 424 | 525 | 626 | 727 | 828 | 929 | 1221 |
| 33 | 131 | 232 | 333 | 434 | 535 | 636 | 737 | 838 | 939 | 1331 |
| 44 | 141 | 242 | 343 | 444 | 545 | 646 | 747 | 848 | 949 | 1441 |
| 55 | 151 | 252 | 353 | 454 | 555 | 656 | 757 | 858 | 959 | 1551 |
| 66 | 161 | 262 | 363 | 464 | 565 | 666 | 767 | 868 | 969 | 1661 |
| 77 | 171 | 272 | 373 | 474 | 575 | 676 | 777 | 878 | 979 | 1771 |
| 88 | 181 | 282 | 383 | 484 | 585 | 686 | 787 | 888 | 989 | 1881 |
| 99 | 191 | 292 | 393 | 494 | 595 | 696 | 797 | 898 | 999 | 1991 |

- Do all numerical palindromes have an even-digit sum? Can you see any pattern in the sum of the digits for palindromic dates?

# FISHING

**Initial Graph...**
Circle the number that tells how many fish you have caught so far this year.

| | | | | | | | | | |
|---|---|---|---|---|---|---|---|---|---|
| 1 | 2 | 3 | 4 | 5 | 6 | 7 | 8 | 9 | 10 |
| 11 | 12 | 13 | 14 | 15 | 16 | 17 | 18 | 19 | 20 |
| 21 | 22 | 23 | 24 | 25 | 26 | 27 | 28 | 29 | 30 |
| 31 | 32 | 33 | 34 | 35 | 36 | 37 | 38 | 39 | 40 |
| 41 | 42 | 43 | 44 | 45 | 46 | 47 | 48 | 49 | 50 |
| 51 | 52 | 53 | 54 | 55 | 56 | 57 | 58 | 59 | 60 |
| 61 | 62 | 63 | 64 | 65 | 66 | 67 | 68 | 69 | 70 |
| 71 | 72 | 73 | 74 | 75 | 76 | 77 | 78 | 79 | 80 |
| 81 | 82 | 83 | 84 | 85 | 86 | 87 | 88 | 89 | 90 |
| 91 | 92 | 93 | 94 | 95 | 96 | 97 | 98 | 99 | 100 |

**Speaking of Fishing...**
- Where is the nearest place to go fishing? Does our state have rules about fishing? Is there a limit to the number of fish you can get in one year? Can you only fish at certain times during the year? Do different rules apply to different species of fish?
- Where would your response be if you have caught no fish this year?

**Focus Question...**
- Are the circled answers for the class related in any way?

**Problem...**
Paul likes to fish and has caught several fish this year. The total number of fish he caught was:
- divisible by 3
- even
- less than 40
- a square number

How many fish do you think Paul caught? Can you use a graph like the one above to help you find the answer?

# FISHING

## Objectives
- to construct, read, and interpret tables, charts, and graphs
- to describe and represent relationships with tables, graphs, and rules
- to develop and use order relations for whole numbers, fractions, decimals, integers, and rational numbers

## Graphing
This problem narrows the range of possible integers for the number of fish caught, one step at a time.

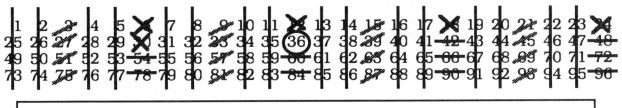

## Mathing
The first fact, *divisible by 3*, limits the table to multiples of three. *Even*, the second fact, limits the table to multiples of two. Combining these into multiples of six (two times three) that are *less than 40* narrows the possibilities to:

6    12    18    24    30    36

The final fact, *a square number*, leaves only one possibility from the selection above: 36 (6 × 6).

## Discussing
Help students devise a method of attacking this problem. *"Does it make a difference which fact you consider first? Does it change your answer? Does it make the problem easier or more difficult? Does it take a longer or shorter time to solve?"*

## Answering
Paul caught 36 fish this year, as the number 36 is the only integer that is divisible by 3, even, less than 40, and also a square.

## Extending
- List several two- and three-digit numbers that are divisible by three. What do you notice about the sum of their digits? Now list several even numbers. Do they have a pattern on a number chart? How about square numbers? Can a pattern be formed by integer sums to form squares (1, 1 + 3 = 4, 1 + 3 + 5 = 9, etc.)?"

- Problems similar to this can be formed by creating a chart of integers, then eliminating sets of numbers one step at a time, as shown above for the preceding problem. As each fact is introduced, eliminated sets of numbers are crossed off. Continue eliminating numbers by observing the numbers that have not been crossed off and introducing a new fact that eliminates part of that set.

  Facts can include primes, sum of digits, powers of two, even, odd, factors, multiples, less than or greater than, comparison of digits by place value, and so on. Once students see how problems of this type can be created by the elimination method, they will enjoy formulating problems for others to solve.

# BUILDING A NUMBER

**Initial Graph...**
Think of the street number on your house. Mark the graph to the right of the last digit of your house's street number.

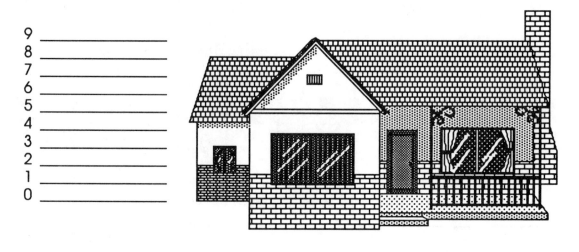

```
9 _____
8 _____
7 _____
6 _____
5 _____
4 _____
3 _____
2 _____
1 _____
0 _____
```

**Speaking of House Numbers...**
- Why do we need house numbers? Do you get to choose your own? If not, who assigns them? What method do they use? Are house numbers chosen at random?
- What is the street address of our school? Estimate the number of homes along this street. How did you arrive at that estimate? How could you check your answer?

**Focus Question...**
- How many digits do most homes in this neighborhood have? How many different street (house) numbers can be made from the digits 1 and 2? How many from the digits 1, 2, and 3?

**Problem...**
After a storm, Rosita found the digit signs for the street number of her house scattered on the ground. How many different four-digit numbers could she make using each of the following digits?

# BUILDING A NUMBER

## Objectives
- to describe, extend, analyze, and create a wide variety of patterns
- to systematically collect, organize, and describe data
- to model situations by constructing a sample space to determine probabilities

## Graphing
One strategy for problem solving is to make a list of possible solutions. Forming a list of four-digit numbers using digits 9, 6, 8, and 1 can be done directly on a class graph. Place a different number on each line. List all possibilities keeping the thousands place constant.

| | | | |
|---|---|---|---|
| 9681 | 6981 | 8961 | 1968 |
| 9618 | 6918 | 8916 | 1986 |
| 9861 | 6891 | 8691 | 1698 |
| 9816 | 6819 | 8619 | 1689 |
| 9186 | 6198 | 8196 | 1896 |
| 9168 | 6189 | 8169 | 1869 |

## Mathing
Look at each place value. There are four possible choices for the thousands digit. Once that has been written, there are three remaining choices for the hundreds place, two then remain for the tens place, and, finally, one for the units place. Thus, the number of possibilities would be: $4 \times 3 \times 2 \times 1 = 24$.

## Discussing
When the list is complete, ask questions about the four-digit numbers. *"Which number has the lowest value? How many numbers are even? How many numbers are divisible by 3? How many numbers are greater than 1900?"*

## Answering
There are 24 different four-digit numbers possible using digits 9, 6, 8, and 1 (see above).

## Extending
- What would happen to the number of possible combinations if two of the digits were the same, i.e., 9, 6, 9, 1? What if three digits were the same?
- Vary the number of place values but keep all four digits. For example, how many different three-digit numbers can be made using the digits 9, 6, 8, and 1?

# ROUNDING

**Initial Graph...**
Study the following diagram and mark your response.

|  | I have planted a garden | I have never planted a garden |
|---|---|---|
| I like fresh vegetables |  |  |
| I do not like fresh vegetables |  |  |

**Speaking of Seeds...**
- How much area do you think you need to plant one carrot, tomato, or corn seed?  Are the necessary areas the same?  Why or why not?
- Can seeds be planted close to each other and still grow to maturity?  How far apart should sunflower seeds be planted?  Do larger plants require a greater amount of planting space?  If you needed to know how much space to leave between seeds, where could you find out?
- Does the size of the seed have any relationship to the size of the mature plant?  In other words, do larger plants have larger seeds?  Do larger plants require a longer time to develop?

**Focus Question...**
- How are seeds processed before packaging?  How are they counted?  Do all packages have the same number of seeds?  Is the number of seeds shown anywhere on the outside of each package?

**Problem...**
Iris works in a seed-packaging plant.  It is her job to stamp the outside of each package with the number of seeds it holds, rounded to the nearest hundred.  For example, if there are 322 seeds in the package, she stamps "300" on the outside.  If there are 298 seeds, she also stamps "300" on the outside.

What is the smallest number of seeds which, when rounded to the nearest hundred, is equal to 300?  Use this graph as a number line to show your answer.

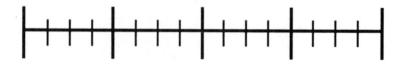

# ROUNDING

## Objectives
- to develop number sense for whole numbers, integers, and rational numbers
- to represent numerical relationships in one- and two-dimensional graphs
- to develop and use order relations for whole numbers, integers, and rational numbers

## Graphing
Use whole numbers on a number line to help students understand the concept of rounding. When rounding is to occur in the tens place, multiples of ten are emphasized. Consider the whole numbers between sixty and seventy:

$$\bullet \ \cdot \ \cdot \ \cdot \ \cdot \ \cdot \ \cdot \ \cdot \ \cdot \ \cdot \ \bullet$$
$$60 \ \ 61 \ \ 62 \ \ 63 \ \ 64 \ \ 65 \ \ 66 \ \ 67 \ \ 68 \ \ 69 \ \ 70$$

Associating rounding with the closest or nearest tens place can be shown as distance along the line. The distance from 62 to 60 is shorter than the distance from 62 to 70. That is why 62 rounds to 60 when rounded to the nearest tens place. However, 65 is the same distance from 60 as it is from 70. By conventional standards, however, half-way rounds up.

When rounding to the nearest hundred, the number line emphasizes each 100:

$$\bullet \ \cdot \ \cdot \ \cdot \ \cdot \ \cdot \ \cdot \ \cdot \ \bullet$$
$$200 \ \ 225 \ \ 250 \ \ 275 \ \ 300 \ \ 325 \ \ 350 \ \ 375 \ \ 400$$

In this case, numbers rounded to 300 would include 250,251,252 • • • 347,348,349.

## Discussing
Ask students how they would feel if they thought they were buying 300 seeds and found only 250 seeds in the package? *"Would you complain? If so, would you direct your complaint to the seed company or to the store where you bought the seeds? What if your package was stamped '300' and you found 349 seeds in it? Should you send the extra 49 seeds back? Would you?"*

Ask students to think of times, places, or jobs where people might use rounding in daily life. Help them distinguish among the amount of rounding commonly used and accepted in various businesses. *"If one wanted to tell how many trees were in a woods, would they say 'exactly 823' or 'approximately 800'? When tax is calculated on a purchase, what happens if it doesn't come out evenly? Do merchants raise or lower the amount to the closest dollar, quarter, dime, nickel, or penny? When going through the supermarket, do you estimate the amount of your purchases before the clerk rings up the exact price? When you see mileage shown on a road map, are the exact number of miles indicated?"*

## Answering
When rounding to the nearest hundred, the smallest number of seeds which rounds to 300 would be 250.

## Extending
- What is the largest whole number which, when rounded to the nearest hundred, is equal to 300? What is the largest whole number which, when rounded to the nearest ten, is equal to 300?
- Have students make up original problems involving rounding. Make them available for members of the class to solve.

# GUESSING HOW MANY JAWBREAKERS

**Initial Graph...**
Study the diagram. Mark your response with a check mark in the circle.

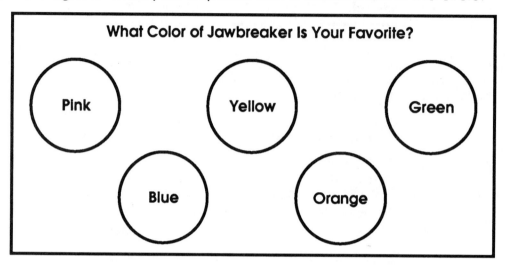

**Speaking of Jawbreakers...**
- Are most jawbreakers the same diameter? If you wanted to fill a jar with jawbreakers, how would the diameter of the jawbreakers affect the number you could get in the jar?
- If 22 jawbreakers will fit in a tall, skinny pint jar, how many will fit in a short, fat pint jar?
- When might you estimate the number of items in a container? What strategies do you use to try to estimate the number?

**Focus Question...**
- How many jawbreakers might fit in a pint jar? If the actual count is 22, how far off was your estimate?

**Problem...**
The Sweethome Drug Store had a contest. They filled a jar with jawbreakers and whoever came closest to guessing the number of jawbreakers in the jar got a new radio.

Candace tried to estimate the weight of the jar, then made a guess of 650 jawbreakers, which was 120 off the actual count. Basil tried to count the jawbreakers around the bottom of the jar and estimate the number of layers. He finally guessed 500—which was only 30 off. How many jawbreakers were really in the jar? Can you make a graph to help you with the answer?

# GUESSING HOW MANY JAWBREAKERS

## Objectives
- to develop number sense for whole numbers, integers, and rational numbers
- to construct, read, and interpret tables, charts, and graphs
- to develop and use order relations for whole numbers, integers, and rational numbers

## Graphing
One method of justification is to mark the two guesses on a number line and surround each point with two possible answers by adding and subtracting the "amounts off" and finding out which ones correspond.

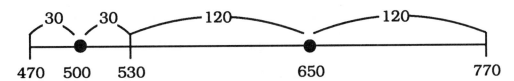

## Mathing
Some students may start with just one guess, let's say the guess of 650, and realize that the answer must be 120 away from that (530 or 770), then transfer to the other guess and decide if one of those values is within the range of "30 away from 500."

Many students realize that the true value of the number of jawbreakers must lie between the two guesses, as neither "amount off" was greater than the difference between the two original guesses. Hence, they could add 30 to the lower guess of 500, or they could subtract 120 from the higher guess of 650.

## Discussing
*"What if Candace had made a guess of 650 and Basil had guessed 500, and both were off the actual count by the same amount? Then, what would the actual number of jawbreakers have been? Could you graph your answer? When people estimate the number of objects in a jar, do they generally overestimate or underestimate? Is it easier to estimate the number of large objects in a large jar, small objects in a small jar, or small objects in a large jar? Why do you think so?"*

## Answering
There were 530 jawbreakers in the jar.

## Extending
- What if the actual number of jawbreakers lie in a range outside of the difference between the two guesses? For example, if the guesses had been 600 (132 off) and 673 (59 off), could you still determine the actual number of jawbreakers?
- Suppose one guess had been twice as far from the real number of jawbreakers as the other guess. Then how many jawbreakers were there? Is more than one answer possible?

# DIGITS IN PHONE NUMBERS

**Initial Graph...**
Caleb's phone number is 582-3148.  The sum of the last two digits is 12 (4 + 8).
What is the sum of the last two digits of your phone number?  Place an **X** after
the number below that corresponds to this sum.

### Sum of last two digits in your phone number

| | | | |
|---|---|---|---|
| 0 | | 11 | |
| 1 | | 12 | |
| 2 | | 13 | |
| 3 | | 14 | |
| 4 | | 15 | |
| 5 | | 16 | |
| 6 | | 17 | |
| 7 | | 18 | |
| 8 | | 19 | |
| 9 | | 20 | |
| 10 | | 21 | |

**Speaking of Phone Numbers...**
- Do you think that the first two digits of a phone number are random?  What
  about the last three digits?  If not, what determines these numbers?  How
  could you find out?
- Are there certain digits reserved for businesses?
- How many students have phone numbers that are even?  Odd?  Prime?

**Focus Question...**
- Would a graph of the very last digit of phone numbers show randomness?

**Problem...**
If you add the last two digits of telephone numbers, will certain sums always
appear more frequently than others in any phone book?  If so, what are they?
What makes you think they will be more common?  Can you test your answer
without adding all the numbers in all the phone books?  How?  Make a graph
to support your answer.

 © 1990 Midwest Publications • Critical Thinking Press & Software, P.O. Box 448, Pacific Grove, CA  93950

# DIGITS IN PHONE NUMBERS

## Objectives
- to develop, analyze, and explain methods for solving proportions
- to describe, extend, analyze, and create a wide variety of patterns
- to describe and represent relationships with tables, graphs, and rules
- to systematically collect, organize, and describe data
- to construct, read, and interpret tables, charts, and graphs

## Materials
An old telephone book (white pages)

## Mathing
To add more data to the graph, tear random pages from an old phone book and give one page to each student. Ask them to add the last two digits of each phone number on their pages and record the results of their efforts on their own graph. (You may want to set a time limit or ask each student to do a single column.)

## Graphing
The class graph should take on the appearance of a bell curve. Emphasize the pattern by cutting out the strip of Xs from each student's graph and sticking them onto a single class graph. The bell curve will begin to take shape as more results are added to the graph.

## Discussing
Note that there are more ways to make a sum of 5 (0 + 5, 1 + 4, 2 + 3, 3 + 2, 4 + 1, 5 + 0) than a sum of 0 (0 + 0). Sums 19, 20, and 21 are impossible. Should 9 or 10 have the greater number of responses? Ask the class to chart the different combinations for the sums 0–18 by placing combinations to the left of the sums, as shown below. They should then graph the sums to the right. A similar shape should appear on both sides.

| LAST TWO DIGITS | | | | | | | | | | SUM | |
|---|---|---|---|---|---|---|---|---|---|---|---|
| | | | | | | | | | 00 | 0 | |
| | | | | | | | | 01 | 10 | 1 | |
| | | | | | | | 02 | 11 | 20 | 2 | |
| | | | | | | 03 | 12 | 21 | 30 | 3 | |
| | | | | | 04 | 13 | 22 | 31 | 40 | 4 | |
| | | | | 05 | 14 | 23 | 32 | 41 | 50 | 5 | |
| | | | 06 | 15 | 24 | 33 | 42 | 51 | 60 | 6 | |
| | | 07 | 16 | 25 | 34 | 43 | 52 | 61 | 70 | 7 | |
| | 08 | 17 | 26 | 35 | 44 | 53 | 62 | 71 | 80 | 8 | |
| 09 | 18 | 27 | 36 | 45 | 54 | 63 | 72 | 81 | 90 | 9 | S |
| | 19 | 28 | 37 | 46 | 55 | 64 | 73 | 82 | 91 | 10 | |
| | | 29 | 38 | 47 | 56 | 65 | 74 | 83 | 92 | 11 | U |
| | | | 39 | 48 | 57 | 66 | 75 | 84 | 93 | 12 | |
| | | | | 49 | 58 | 67 | 76 | 85 | 94 | 13 | M |
| | | | | | 59 | 68 | 77 | 86 | 95 | 14 | |
| | | | | | | 69 | 78 | 87 | 96 | 15 | |
| | | | | | | | 79 | 88 | 97 | 16 | |
| | | | | | | | | 89 | 98 | 17 | |
| | | | | | | | | | 99 | 18 | |

## Answering
The graph above shows the frequency of sums, with 9 having the greatest response.

## Extending
Percents are easy to use in this problem, as there are exactly 100 combinations to make the different sums. Thus 10% of the answers should have a sum of 9, 9% a sum of 10 or 8, 8% a sum of 11 or 7, and so on. Did the class have any "total's row" that agreed with the statistical percentage? How far off were their answers?

# ADDING PAGE NUMBERS

**Initial Graph...**
This book is turned to page 15. If the pages follow each other in the normal way, what is the sum of this page and the one that follows? Mark your answer with an **X** on the number line below.

10 11 12 13 14 15 16 17 18 19 20 21 22 23 24 25 26 27 28 29 30 31 32 33 34 35 36

**Speaking of Page Numbers...**
- How could you determine the page someone is on in a book if you only knew the sum of that page and the following page?
- If I gave you a sum of 19 for two consecutive pages, could you find the beginning page number? Can you show it two different ways?
- Is it possible to have a sum of 19 for three consecutive pages? Why or why not? What sums are possible for three pages that follow each other?

**Focus Question...**
- Is is possible to have a sum of 19 for four consecutive pages? Which sums are possible for four pages?

**Problem...**
Werner noticed that the sum of the page numbers of four special pages of drawings in his favorite book is 98. If the pages follow each other, on what page do the drawings begin?

# ADDING PAGE NUMBERS

## Objectives
- to generalize solutions and strategies to new problem situations
- to develop number sense for whole numbers, integers, and rational numbers
- to develop and use order relations for whole numbers, integers, and rational numbers
- to analyze tables and graphs to identify properties and relationships
- to apply algebraic methods to solve a variety of real-world and mathematical problems

## Graphing
Students can demonstrate the answer using a long paper or line with a length of 98 or more units. If they accordian fold the length, with the first fold on unit 23, and each successive fold point extending one unit over the linear length of the previous fold, the final fold will occur on unit 98. (The illustration shows the top view of the folded paper placed on edge.)

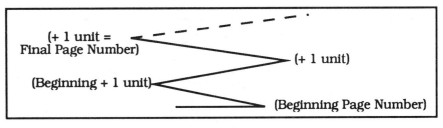

## Mathing
Some students will try to divide the 98 into four sections, giving an approximate 24, then estimate the first page to be 24. However, 24 + 25 + 26 + 27 = 102, which is too much. Therefore they might try the beginning page to be one lower, which is 23, and 23 + 24 + 25 + 26 = 98. They have then reached the right answer by first estimating then reducing.

This is also a good problem for visualizing a number, increasing that number by 1, 2, 3, then obtaining a sum of 98:

> beginning page number
> beginning page number + 1
> beginning page number + 2
> beginning page number + 3
> 4 × (beginning page number) + 6 = 98
> 4 × (beginning page number) = 92
> beginning page number = 23

## Discussing
Whatever method students use, ask them to justify their answers. *"Can you see any patterns to adding four consecutive numbers? How do the patterns change if you use only odd or even page numbers?"*

## Answering
The drawings began on page 23.

## Extending
- During his lunch hour, Werner read a 20-page chapter from a book. The sum of the first and last pages he read was 105. What was the number of the last page of that chapter?
- Werner needs to buy 57 yards of material for his three sisters, each of whom will receive a different amount to go with the patterns they picked out. Amy needed one yard more than Sue, and Sue needed one yard more than Peggy. How many yards of material should each daughter receive?

# TOPS IN BASEBALL

**Initial Graph...**
Study the diagram and mark your response.

**Speaking of Baseball...**
- What country developed baseball? What rules does the game have? Have they changed during the past few years? If so, how and why? How could you find out?
- Has technology changed the ball? The bat? The gloves? If so, how?
- Show me two ways to pitch a ball. Are there different ways to bat? How many? Which way of pitching or batting is most popular? How can you find out? What could you do with this information if you were the manager of a baseball team?

**Focus Question...**
- How are baseball scores recorded in a newspaper? What do the different parts of a "box score" stand for? Is there always a winner in a baseball game? What determines who wins? How could you tell who won a baseball tournament?

**Problem...**
Felix plays baseball. His team is one of sixteen teams that will play in the city tournament. When any team loses one game, it will be out of the tournament. Assuming there are no tie games, how many games will be played before the winner can be announced?

Can you use a graph to help you find the answer? Use an **X** to stand for a team that is still in the tournament. For example, sixteen **X**s would stand for the sixteen teams in the first round of the city tournament.

# TOPS IN BASEBALL

### Objectives
- to develop number sense for whole numbers
- to formulate problems from situations within and outside mathematics
- to explore problems and describe results using graphical, numerical, physical, algebraic, and verbal mathematical models or representations

### Graphing
Students can justify their answer in many ways, including a branching diagram like the one shown below, commonly used for tournament or elimination schedules, or by marking out alternate **X**s (to indicate the losing team in each game) and counting the marks. Ask students what graphic elements they could count in these diagrams that would tell them the number of games played (vertical lines; "V-shapes").

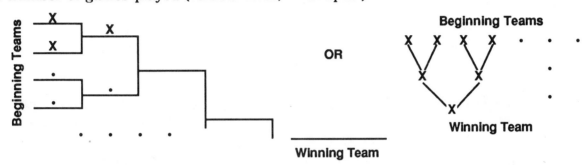

### Mathing
Answers may be justified mathematically by considering the number of games in each round. Remember that each game involves two teams.

| | | | | | |
|---|---|---|---|---|---|
| Beginning Round | 16 | teams | → | 8 | games |
| Second Round | 8 | teams | → | 4 | games |
| Third Round | 4 | teams | → | 2 | games |
| Final Round | 2 | teams | → | <u>1</u> | <u>game</u> |
| | | | | 15 | games total |

### Discussing
Ask students to demonstrate and justify their answers. *"Do you notice a pattern? Is there a relationship between the number of teams and the number of games in a single-elimination tournament like the one in the problem? Is there another way you could graph the information to show the answer? What other information can you get from your graph?"*

### Answering
Fifteen (15) games would be played in a single-elimination tournament with 16 teams.

### Extending
- What if there had been 100 teams in such a tournament? Is there a formula you could use to find the number of games necessary for any even number of beginning teams?

| <u>Teams</u> | <u>Games</u> |
|---|---|
| 2 | 1 |
| 4 | 3 |
| 6 | 5 |
| • | • |
| $n$ (even) | $n-1$ |

- How would an odd number of beginning teams change this pattern?

# WEIGHT OF A CAN

**Initial Graph...**
If you needed to fasten two pieces of wood together, what would you use?
Choose one of the objects listed below and mark your choice on its line.

| | |
|---:|---|
| **Safety Pin** | _____ |
| **Glue** | _____ |
| **Nail** | _____ |
| **Bolt** | _____ |
| **Zipper** | _____ |

**Speaking of Fasteners...**
- What do all of the above items have in common?
- What might one build that would require a nail? Where might you use a nail and glue together?
- How long ago did man invent nails? What did the first nails look like? What were they used for? How have nails changed over the years? Where could you find information about nails?
- If a nail is left outside on the ground, might any animal try to eat it? Which animals? How would a nail affect an animal that ate it? Could a nail on the ground be dangerous to anything else? How or why?
- What are the similarities and differences between a nail and a bolt? Between a safety pin and a zipper? Between a zipper and glue?
- Do you have any nails at home? What kinds and what do you use them for? How do you store them?

**Focus Question...**
- Where can you buy nails? How are they sold? Are all nails the same size?

**Problem...**
Penny bought a can of nails at the hardware store. The can held 30 nails, and the can and nails together weighed 263 ounces.

On her way home Penny dropped the can and spilled 15 nails onto the ground. After she got home, she weighed the can (with 15 fewer nails) again, and it weighed 143 ounces. What would the empty can weigh? Make a graph that justifies your answer.

# WEIGHT OF A CAN

## Objectives
- to generalize solutions and strategies to new problem situations
- to reflect on and clarify thinking about mathematical ideas and situations
- to represent situations and number patterns with tables, graphs, verbal rules, and equations and to explore the interrelationships of these representations
- to compute with whole numbers, integers, and rational numbers

## Graphing
The weight of the nails can be separated from the weight of the can by linear representation (below). The nails can then be graphically divided in half.

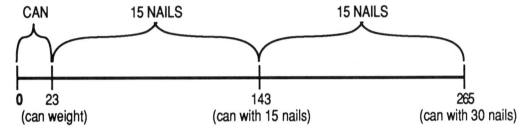

## Mathing
Some students may begin by working with the difference between the two weights; others may notice that half of the nails were lost and concentrate on the half that remains inside the can.

If half of the nails are gone, students can determine the difference in weight:

$$\begin{array}{r} 263 \quad \text{(original weight)} \\ \underline{-143 \quad \text{(remaining weight)}} \\ 120 \quad \text{ounces (weight of 15 missing nails)} \end{array}$$

This means that the 30 original nails weighed 240 ounces (15 nails weigh 120 ounces). Hence, the weight of the can is determined from either the first or the second weighing of the can by subtracting the weight of the nails:

$$\begin{array}{ccc} 263 & \text{or} & 143 \\ \underline{-240} & & \underline{-120} \\ 23 & & 23 \end{array}$$

## Discussing
Help students focus on various aspects of the problem. *"What was the total weight with the can and all the nails? How did that weight compare after 15 nails were spilled onto the ground? What part of the total number of nails was spilled? Would the problem change if only 8 nails had been spilled instead of 15?"*

## Answering
The empty can (with no nails) weighs 23 ounces.

## Extending
Another can of nails weighed 124.5 ounces and contained 20 nails. One-fourth of these nails were used to build a dog house. The can of remaining nails weighed 107 ounces. What was the weight of each individual nail?

# VALUE OF YOUR FAVORITE SPORT

**Initial Graph...**
Write the name of your favorite sport on the line below.

_____

**Speaking of Sports...**
- Which sport is most popular in your classroom?  Can you think of any sports that were not named at all?
- Can you think of the name of any professional teams that play any of the sports listed?  What do these sports have in common?  How do they differ?
- What are the rules of the third sport on the list?  How long has that sport been around?  How can you find out if you don't know?

_____

**Focus Question...**
- How many letters are in the name of each sport named by the class?  Do any have the same number?  Do any contain one of the first five letters of the alphabet?  Do any contain one of the last five letters of the alphabet?

_____

**Problem...**
Look at the name of your favorite sport and the letters in its name.  If A = 1¢, B = 2¢, C = 3¢, ..., Z = 26¢, what is the value of the name of your favorite sport?

| | | | | | |
|---|---|---|---|---|---|
| A = 1 | B = 2 | C = 3 | D = 4 | E = 5 | F = 6 |
| G = 7 | H = 8 | I = 9 | J = 10 | K = 11 | L = 12 |
| M = 13 | N = 14 | O = 15 | P = 16 | Q = 17 | R = 18 |
| S = 19 | T = 20 | U = 21 | V = 22 | W = 23 | X = 24 |
| | | Y = 25 | Z = 26 | | |

**Example:**　　**HOCKEY = 67¢**　　　8(H) + 15(O) + 3(C) + 11(K) + 5(E) + 25(Y)

| Value | |
|---|---|
| 01–10¢ value | |
| 11–20¢ value | |
| 21–30¢ value | |
| 31–40¢ value | |
| 41–50¢ value | |
| 51–60¢ value | |
| 61–70¢ value | |
| 71–80¢ value | |
| value > 80¢ | |

# VALUE OF YOUR FAVORITE SPORT

## Objectives
- to develop number sense for whole numbers, integers, and rational numbers
- to compute with whole numbers, integers, and rational numbers
- to systematically collect, organize, and describe data

## Discussing
List the chosen sports on the chalkboard. Before students attack the problem statement, ask them to predict which sport will have the highest value on the chart. Can they predict the sport with the lowest value? On what did they base their predictions?

## Mathing
When students have completed their computations, have them write the name of their sport in the appropriate category on a class graph.

## Graphing
Ask questions to help the students compare the values on the class graph. *"Are there several different sports in one value range? Which value range has the greatest number of different sports? Is there any sport whose name has a value greater than $2.00? Which sport has the lowest value? Are any lower than 10¢? Does the way you identify the sport have any bearing on its value? For example, would there be a difference between 'swim' and 'swimming' or between 'roller skating' and 'skating'?"*

Ask the students to create a graph that shows the comparative values of those sports chosen by the class. If they added each sport's value the number of times it was chosen, could they determine which sport had the most "class value"?

## Answering
Answers will vary with the sports.

## Extending
Extend the activity to words other than sports' names. Use some of the following ideas to get started, then think of other areas that might be fun to explore. Help the students discuss data-gathering means and devices before they begin.
- What is the value of the average word?
- What is the value of the average color?
- Who can find the "cheapest" word?
- Can anyone find a word worth more than $1.50?
- Using the names in this class, how do the values of last names compare with the values of first names?
- Whose name in this class has the highest value?
- Who has the "most valuable" pet (breed or type)?
- Whose pet's name is "most valuable"?
- What is the "most valuable" vegetable name?
- What is the "most valuable" car name?
- Can anyone make a $3.00 sentence?

## MARBLES

**Initial Graph...**
Study the diagram and mark your response.

| I FIND IT HARDEST TO: | | |
|---|---|---|
| **Spin a marble** | **Roll a marble** | **Throw a marble** |
| | | |

**Speaking of Marbles...**
- What games have you used marbles for? What rules do those games have? Do they have any rules in common?
- How do you make a marble spin? Is it possible for a marble to roll and spin at the same time? Would different types of marbles roll or spin in different ways? Would oil on the outside of a marble affect its roll or spin? How?
- How far can a marble roll on carpet? On sand? On a waxed floor? Are the distances different? Why?
- What shape is a marble? Why do pebbles on a beach form a marble shape? What makes them different from pebbles that you might find in a field, for example?
- How does a pencil roll differently from a marble? Could you roll a log or an orange around a tree to the other side? How?

**Focus Question...**
- If you wanted to roll a marble near a sitting target, how would you do that? What other objects might roll as accurately as marbles?

**Problem...**
Antonia and Evanna like to shoot marbles. They draw a circle and put a rock at the center, then each shoots a marble from the outside of the circle to see who can come closest to the rock without hitting it. At the end of each round, the loser gives the winner a marble.

Today Antonia has won five games and Evanna has five marbles more than she had when they started to play. Assuming there was a winner for each round, how many rounds did they play? Can you make a graph to help you find the answer?

# MARBLES

## Objectives
- to develop number sense for whole numbers
- to make and analyze tables and graphs to identify properties and relationships
- to model situations using oral, written, concrete, graphical, or algebraic methods

## Graphing
Some students will want to justify immediately with numbers while others will want to act out the problem. The beginning question that arises when acting the rounds is how many marbles each individual has to start. Pick an arbitrary amount, such as 100 marbles each. As rounds are acted out between two students, ask a third to write the number and result of each round on the chalkboard.

| Round | Winner | Evanna | Antonia |
|-------|--------|--------|---------|
| 1 | Evanna | 101 | 99 |
| 2 | Evanna | 102 | 98 |
| 3 | Antonia | 101 | 99 |
| 4 | Antonia | 100 | 100 |
| 5 | Antonia | 99 | 101 |
| 6 | Antonia | 98 | 102 |
| 7 | Evanna | 99 | 101 |
| 8 | Evanna | 100 | 100 |
| 9 | Evanna | 101 | 99 |
| 10 | Evanna | 102 | 98 |
| 11 | Evanna | 103 | 97 |
| 12 | Evanna | 104 | 96 |
| 13 | Antonia | 103 | 97 |
| 14 | Evanna | 104 | 96 |
| 15 | Evanna | 105 | 95 |

Have the class vary the game winner and starting numbers of marbles until they are satisfied that the results of the 15 rounds do not depend upon these quantities.

## Discussing
Use class or group discussion to help students analyze the information they have gathered. *"How many marbles do you think each person had to start? Does it make a difference? Is there any other way you could graph the information to show the answer? Can you draw other conclusions using the information on the graph?"*

## Answering
Evanna and Antonia played 15 rounds of marbles.

## Extending
What if the number of marbles Evanna won and the number of rounds Antonia won changed? If those numbers are always equal, is there a pattern?

| | **Total Rounds** |
|---|---|
| Evanna won 1 marble; Antonia won 1 game | 3 rounds |
| Evanna won 2 marbles; Antonia won 2 games | 6 rounds |
| Evanna won 3 marbles; Antonia won 3 games | 9 rounds |
| •             • | • |
| •             • | • |
| Evanna won $n$ marbles; Antonia won $n$ games | $3n$ rounds |

# A CUT IN SALARY

**Initial Graph...**
Which of these vehicles would you like to own? Mark the diagram to the right to show your choice(s).

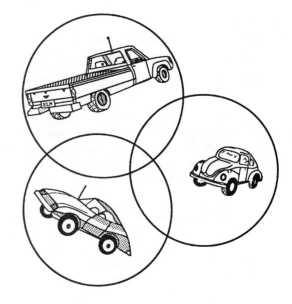

**Speaking of Cars...**
- What would you look for in a car you wanted to buy? What kinds of things would be most important to you? Would these things be most important to everyone why buys a new car?
- Do cars sell better at certain times of the year? When? Why?

**Focus Question...**
- If you were a car salesperson, what might you say to persuade me to buy the truck shown in the **Initial Graph**? One of the other cars?

**Problem...**
Carole got a new part-time job selling cars. It looked good on paper, but at the end of the first week she had sold so few cars that her contract was changed. The salary she was to have received was cut in half, and her boss took out $2 extra to cover other expenses.

There was a holiday during the next week and Carole had trouble getting anyone to even look at the cars, let alone buy them. Once again, her salary was cut in half and $2 was taken out to cover special expenses.

You would think that the third week would have been better, but the stock market fell. People held onto their money, and only one person looked at a car. Carole's salary was cut in half again, and again the boss took an extra $2. She received only $3 for that third week of work—and she certainly couldn't live on that!

What was the original salary on Carole's contract? What kind of graph would help you find the answer?

# A CUT IN SALARY

## Objectives
- to model situations using oral, written, concrete, graphical, and algebraic methods
- to generalize solutions and strategies to new problem situations
- to understand, represent, and use numbers in a variety of equivalent forms (integer, fraction, decimal, percent, exponential, and scientific notation) in real-world and mathematical problem situations
- to understand and apply ratios, proportions, and percents in a wide variety of situations

## Graphing
Consecutive contract salaries could be completed on a chart.

| Contract | Week 1 | Week 2 | Week 3 |
|----------|--------|--------|--------|
| $100.00 | $48.00 | $22.00 | $9.00 |
| 99.00 | 47.50 | 21.75 | 8.875 |
| 98.00 | 47.00 | 21.50 | 8.75 |
| 97.00 | 46.50 | 21.25 | 8.625 |
| • | • | • | • |
| • | • | • | • |

This pattern indicates that for each dollar decrease in the original contract, the third week's salary decreases by twelve and a half cents. The desired result can be found by extending the chart or by establishing and applying a ratio.

## Mathing
An easy method of solving this problem might be to work backward rather than forward. Opposite operations would be needed (i.e., adding two instead of subtracting two, doubling instead of dividing by one half).

$3 (3rd week's salary) + 2 (special expenses) = 5 × 2 = $10.00 (2nd week's salary)

$10 + 2 (special expenses) = 12 × 2 = $24.00 (1st week's salary)

$24 + 2 (special expenses) = 26 × 2 = $52.00 (original contract)

## Discussing
Use class discussion to help students focus on the problem-solving process. *"If you started with a salary of $100, what would your salary be if it were cut in half, then an extra $2 taken out? What would your total loss be, and what would you be left with for a salary the next week? Could you continue by cutting the salary in half the next week and again taking out $2? How does the new total compare to the original $100? Now, let's look at the problem. Carole's original salary is not given. Where could you begin? Is there a way to show Carole's salary with a graph?"*

## Answering
Carole's original salary contract was $52 a week.

## Extending
- What would the original salary have been if the third week's salary was $1.00?
- What other jobs can you think of that pay employees on the basis of what they sell?

# DISTANCE BETWEEN CITIES

### Initial Graph...
If you drove nonstop all day, which of the following would be closest to the total miles you had driven?  Mark an **X** above your answer.

| 1 mile | 10 miles | 100 miles | 1000 miles | 10 000 miles |

### Speaking of Mileage...
- How many cities can we find in this state that everyone in this class has visited?  Are there any cities in any other states that everyone has visited?
- How is mileage recorded on a state map?  Is the distance between all cities recorded?
- From here, what is the closest city in a foreign country?  If you were a bird, how many miles would you have to fly in a straight line to go from here to that city?  How could you find out?

### Focus Question...
- How far is it from here to different nearby cities?  How do you know?  What cities could you drive to in less than one hour?

### Problem...
Patrick lives in Tacoma and would like to visit his friend in Seattle this weekend. He found the following distance information on the map, but he still doesn't know how far it is from Tacoma to Seattle.  Can you help him find out how far he would have to travel?

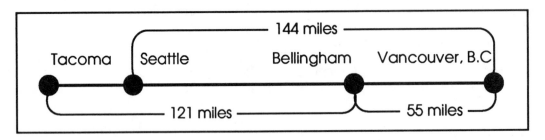

# DISTANCE BETWEEN CITIES

### Objectives
- to model situations using oral, written, concrete, pictorial, and graphical methods
- to acquire confidence in using mathematics meaningfully
- to develop and use order relations for whole numbers, decimals, integers, and rational numbers
- to compute with whole numbers, decimals, integers, and rational numbers
- to extend students' understanding of the process of measurement

### Graphing
Ask students if they can justify their answer on a number line. Are there any other ways to show the answer? What about using strips of paper?

### Mathing
One solution method may be demonstrated by:

   Tacoma to Vancouver, B.C.  = 121 + 55 = 176 miles
   minus Seattle to Vancouver, B.C.    – 144 miles
   Tacoma to Seattle       32 miles

### Discussing
Help the students explore alternative methods of attacking this problem. *"Are there other ways to do this problem? What if the difference between 144 and 55 had been the first mileage taken? What would that difference represent? How might one proceed with the problem from there?"*

### Answering
The distance from Tacoma to Seattle is 32 miles.

### Extending
- The distance from Seattle to Havington is 1229.5 miles. From Seattle to Anderson is 729 miles, from Mobile to Havington is 148 kilometers, and from Winnato to Mobile is 10 miles. How many **kilometers** is it from Anderson to Mobile? Use a diagram like the following to help determine the answer.

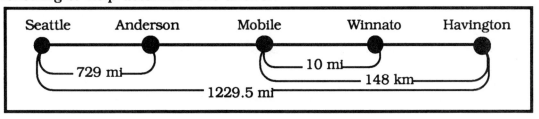

- Find two cities on a local or state map that do **not** have a printed numerical distance between them. How can you find the distance from one of these cities to the other? Share with your classmates how you did this!

# TAKING A TEST

### Initial Graph...
What grade do you expect you will earn on the next test in this class?  Mark your response on the chart below.

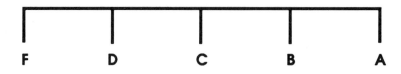

### Speaking of Test Grades...
- What if you expect to earn a B+ on the next test?  Could you mark that grade on the chart above?  If so, where would you make your mark?
- Are test grades the only thing that make up your final class grade?  If not, what else is considered?  Are there some classes in which you get graded without taking tests?  Do you ever take tests that don't "count" toward your grade?
- What is the purpose of tests?  What information does a test give you?  Your teacher?  How can you use information from test results to help yourself?
- Do you usually know what letter grade you got on a test before it has been handed back?  How do you know?
- Would it ever be right to change a letter grade after it has been recorded in the grade book?  If so, under what circumstances?
- Do your test grades in math class accurately reflect your understanding of mathematics?  Why or why not?  What other ways can you think of that would reward **learning** besides letter grades?

### Focus Question...
- How are test grades determined?  Do schools in all counties, states, and countries give letter grades based on the same grade scale?

### Problem...
Reed is taking an advanced science class this semester.  The last test that he took had 100 problems on it.  Letter grades were based on the ranges of correct answers shown in the chart to the right.

Reed answered all the questions and had 26 more answers correct than incorrect.  What was his letter grade?  Can you use a graph to justify your answer?

| A | 90–100 |
|---|--------|
| B | 80–89 |
| C | 70–79 |
| D | 60–69 |
| F | below 60 |

 © 1990 Midwest Publications • Critical Thinking Press & Software, P.O. Box 448, Pacific Grove, CA  93950

# TAKING A TEST

## Objectives
- to represent numerical relationships in one- and two-dimensional graphs
- to develop number sense for whole numbers, integers, and rational numbers
- to develop and use order relations for whole numbers, integers, and rational numbers
- to compute with whole numbers, integers, and rational numbers

## Graphing
A score of 100 may be seen as a line segment 100 units long. Incorrect units would be one section; correct units would be the same distance as incorrect units plus 26 extra units.

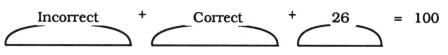

That leaves a remainder of 74 units (100 – 26) to be divided in half.

## Mathing
Mathematical justification could be demonstrated by either of these methods.

100 (total questions) – 26 (difference between correct and incorrect answers) = 74, then:
>    half of the 74 are incorrect = 37 incorrect answers, and
>    100 questions – 37 incorrect answers = 63 correct answers

**OR**

>    half of the 74 are correct = 37 correct answers, and
>    37 correct answers + 26 correct answers = 63 correct answers

## Discussing
*"Consider a test of 100 questions where Reed answers the same number correct as incorrect. What would his score be? What would his score be if he had one more answer correct?"* Continue this process until students see a pattern develop.

| Score (correct) | Incorrect | Difference |
|:---:|:---:|:---:|
| 50 | 50 | 0 |
| 51 | 49 | 2 |
| 52 | 48 | 4 |
| 53 | 47 | 6 |
| ... | ... | ... |

Help them extend the pattern. *"When does this pattern reach a difference of 26? What would the score be then?"*

## Answering
With a score of 63, Reed's letter grade would have been D.

## Extending
- The next biology test also had 100 problems and the same grading scale. This time, however, partial credit was given for work attempted. Reed answered all the questions and had 16 more answers correct than incorrect. The teacher gave him half-credit for half of his incorrect answers. What was his grade on this test?
- On the third 100-problem test, the biology teacher took off one-fourth of a point for unanswered problems. Reed had 73 correct answers, 19 incorrect answers, and left the rest of the problems unanswered. What was his score on this test?

# PRICE OF AN APPLE

**Problem...**
Amos paid 79 cents a pound for the apple on the desk. How much do you think this one apple cost him? Mark your response on the graph below.

## Cost, in cents, of one apple

| | | | | |
|---|---|---|---|---|
| 1 | 26 | 51 | 76 | 101 |
| 2 | 27 | 52 | 77 | 102 |
| 3 | 28 | 53 | 78 | 103 |
| 4 | 29 | 54 | 79 | 104 |
| 5 | 30 | 55 | 80 | 105 |
| 6 | 31 | 56 | 81 | 106 |
| 7 | 32 | 57 | 82 | 107 |
| 8 | 33 | 58 | 83 | 108 |
| 9 | 34 | 59 | 84 | 109 |
| 10 | 35 | 60 | 85 | 110 |
| 11 | 36 | 61 | 86 | 111 |
| 12 | 37 | 62 | 87 | 112 |
| 13 | 38 | 63 | 88 | 113 |
| 14 | 39 | 64 | 89 | 114 |
| 15 | 40 | 65 | 90 | 115 |
| 16 | 41 | 66 | 91 | 116 |
| 17 | 42 | 67 | 92 | 117 |
| 18 | 43 | 68 | 93 | 118 |
| 19 | 44 | 69 | 94 | 119 |
| 20 | 45 | 70 | 95 | 120 |
| 21 | 46 | 71 | 96 | 121 |
| 22 | 47 | 72 | 97 | 122 |
| 23 | 48 | 73 | 98 | 123 |
| 24 | 49 | 74 | 99 | 124 |
| 25 | 50 | 75 | 100 | 125 |

# PRICE OF AN APPLE

## Objectives
- to use computation, estimation, and proportions to solve problems
- to use estimation to check the reasonableness of results
- to develop, analyze, and explain computation procedures and estimation techniques

## Materials
One average-sized apple, placed where all students can see it; scales for weighing the apple

## Graphing
A two-dimensional graph of weight and cost (shown to the right) will show prices for all fractional parts of a pound.

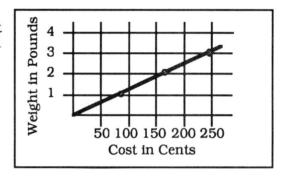

## Discussing
How did students proceed in arriving at a price? Encourage them to discuss a variety of methods, then assess the accuracy of each. Some might say they lifted the apple, estimated its weight, then estimated the part or parts of 79 cents per pound. Others may justify their answer by saying that the apple looks smaller, larger, or the same size as those in a vending machine and that they adjusted the price accordingly. Still others may not even pick up the apple, but will assume that one apple weighs one pound and estimate the cost at 79¢. Other possibilities may include knowing the price of a full bag of apples and trying to divide the price per bag to get their result or comparing the weight with a known weight, such as a book or rock or pound of hamburger, and go from there.

Whatever method students use, they should explain their process, as that is more important than the final answer. The actual price may then be demonstrated step by step as you weigh the apple and figure the price per pound by the known weight.

## Answering
The answer varies with each apple, but most apples will weigh between ¼ and ½ pound, thus the cost would fall between 20–40¢.

## Extending
- What is the cost of the edible part of this apple? What about the cost of the core? How many different ways can you think of that would help you find out? Can you do it without eating any of the apple?
- Assume that three apples of different sizes are sold at 49¢ per pound. Estimate the cost of each apple, then weigh each and figure its price. Did you underestimate or overestimate? How far off were your estimates? How much would all three apples cost together?

# SECTIONS IN AN ORANGE

**Problem...**
Laverne wants to eat the orange on the desk. Before she gets a chance to do this, can you estimate the number of sections in the orange? Mark your estimate on the chart below.

| Sections | |
|---|---|
| 1 | |
| 2 | |
| 3 | |
| 4 | |
| 5 | |
| 6 | |
| 7 | |
| 8 | |
| 9 | |
| 10 | |
| 11 | |
| 12 | |
| 13 | |
| 14 | |
| 15 | |
| 16 | |
| 17 | |
| 18 | |
| 19 | |
| 20 | |
| >20 | |

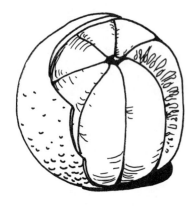
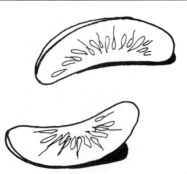

# SECTIONS IN AN ORANGE

## Objectives
- to use an unseen quantity to graph results which begin to make a statistical average
- to systematically collect, organize, and describe data
- to construct, read, and interpret tables, charts, and graphs
- to make inferences and convincing arguments based on data analysis

## Materials
An orange, placed where students can see it, and 1 orange for every 2 students in the class

## Graphing
Distribute oranges to the class. Ask the students to peel their orange, count the sections, then record their results on a class graph.

## Discussing
There is no reason for a student to know the actual number of sections in any orange. However, several (20–30) oranges can be used to show an average.

As the class graph develops, ask questions that encourage students to draw inferences from the data they have collected. *"Does the graph display a pattern after five oranges have been counted? After ten oranges? After all the class's oranges? Does the class graph indicate an average that would provide a better estimate if students were given this problem again?"*

Students' guesses on the number of sections may be based upon the size of the orange or the brand it is. The actual counting techniques of the orange sections need to be discussed with the group. Hopefully, students will come up with counting methods using group cooperation rather than individual counting.

## Answering
The average orange contains about eight sections.

## Extending
- Estimate the number of seeds in a pumpkin. Are the number of seeds in a pumpkin related to the size of the pumpkin?
- Graph other gathered data, i.e., the number of petals on a rose, seeds on pine cones, scales on pine cones, seeds in a watermelon, or seeds in an apple.
- Use the results to calculate the **mode** (most frequent number of orange sections), the **median** (middle number of orange sections if all were lined up according to sections), and the **mean** (calculated average by adding total sections and dividing into the total number of oranges). See the "Statistics" chapter for further explanation of these types of averages.

# AGE IN SECONDS

**Problem...**
Millie says she is over 30 million seconds old.  How many seconds old would
you estimate you were at midnight last night?  Mark your estimate on the
number line below.

**Millions of Seconds**

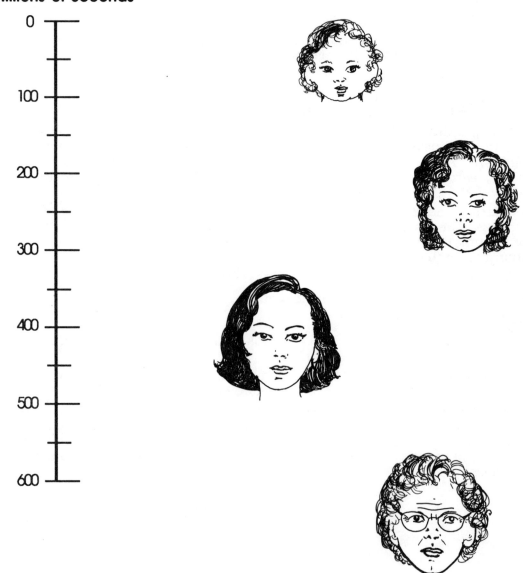

# AGE IN SECONDS

## Objectives

- to use computation, estimation, and proportions to solve problems
- to understand, represent, and use numbers in a variety of equivalent forms (integer, fraction, decimal, percent, exponential, and scientific notation) in real-world and mathematical problem situations
- to understand and apply ratios, proportions, and percents in a variety of situations

## Graphing

Calculators are a great tool for this exercise. Since the problem as stated is to ***estimate***, rather than calculate, age in seconds, one method might be:

1 year = 60 (sec.) × 60 (min.) × 24 (hrs.) × 365 (days) = 30 million sec. (approx.)

Place a mark (*) on the class graph showing the coordinate (30) for someone aged one. Age two would be approximately 60 million seconds. Add another mark (*) on the graph. Point out that there appears to be an increase of 30 million seconds each year. This increase is represented by the same distance along the number line. Ask students to expand this information graphically to show their own age in seconds.

## Discussing

*"How many seconds are in a minute? How many minutes are in an hour? How can we determine the number of seconds in an hour if we know the above information? If we knew the number of inches in a foot and the number of feet in a yard, could we use a similar method to find the number of inches in a yard? If we knew how many yards were in a football field, could we find the number of inches? How?"*

## Answering

Answers will vary according to the ages of the students. A twelve-year old, for example, would be about 360 million seconds old.

## Expanding

Express the relationship between age in years and age in seconds on a two-dimensional graph. Would the relationship be a straight line?

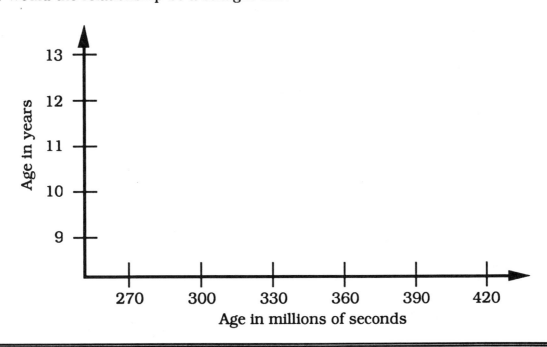

# DAYS IN A MILLION SECONDS

**Problem...**

Akela was wondering how long she would have to wait for one million seconds to pass. Can you estimate the number of days in one million seconds. Make a mark on the line to the right of your estimate.

| Number of Days | |
|---|---|
| 1–100 | |
| 101–500 | |
| 501–1000 | |
| 1001–5000 | |
| 5001–10 000 | |
| 10 001–50 000 | |
| 50 001–100 000 | |
| 100 001–500 000 | |
| > 500 000 | |

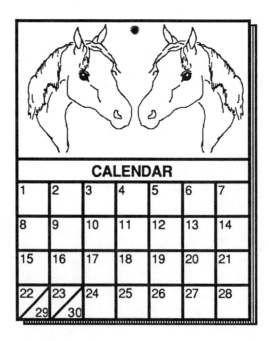

# DAYS IN A MILLION SECONDS

### Objectives
- to develop number sense for whole numbers, integers, and rational numbers
- to explore problems and describe results using graphical, numerical, physical, algebraic, and verbal mathematical models or representations
- to understand how the basic arithmetic operations are related to one another
- to use computation, estimation, and proportions to solve problems

### Graphing
Division may not be readily recognized as the second step involving the total one million seconds. One method of demonstrating that might be to graph a table:

| seconds | days |
|---------|------|
| 85 000 | 1 |
| 170 000 | 2 |
| 255 000 | 3 |
| ••• | ••• |

### Discussing
*"What is greater than a million? For the next few minutes, snap each second and count. ... Are we close to a million? How many thousands are in a million? How many hundreds are in a million? Would it take long for 100 seconds to pass? How could you get "3" days given 255 000 seconds?"* (Divide 255 000 by 85 000. Simplifying the problem this way helps students develop a strategy for finding the number of days for "any" number of seconds.) Ask students to justify their answers on the class graph. You may need to remind them that estimation should include rounding.

### Estimating
Students are frequently at a loss as to which operation to use in problems of this type. Typically, a student might justify that there are 60 seconds in a minute, 60 minutes in an hour, and 24 hours in a day

$$60 \times 60 \times 24 = 85\ 000 \text{ seconds (approximately) for 1 day}$$

$$1\ 000\ 000 \div 85\ 000 = 12 \text{ days (approximately)}$$

There are other methods for estimating answers to this problem. You may find students who start with the 1 000 000 seconds and proceed from there.

$$1\ 000\ 000 \div 60 \text{ (seconds in a minute)} = 16\ 666 \text{ minutes}$$

$$16\ 666 \div 60 \text{ (minutes in an hour)} = 278 \text{ hours}$$

$$278 \div 24 \text{ (hours in a day)} = 12 \text{ days (approximately)}$$

### Answering
There are approximately 12 days in one million seconds. The correct response on the graph would therefore be 1–100 days.

### Extending
- How many days are there in one thousand seconds?
- How many weeks are in one trillion seconds?
- Could you reach another planet if you traveled one million miles?

# KERNELS OF POPCORN

## Initial Graph
Have you ever eaten popcorn?  Did you like it?  Where would your opinion of popcorn belong on this line?  Mark an **X** to show your response.

| I don't like any<br>type of popcorn | I like all types<br>of popcorn |
|---|---|

## Speaking of Popcorn...
- Do all kernels of popcorn weigh the same?  Would you have to weigh every popcorn kernel in the world to find out?  Why or why not?
- How much is 7 grams?  Can you name an object in this room that weighs about 7 grams?
- What happens when popcorn kernels pop?  Does popped corn weigh more, less, or the same as the same number of unpopped kernels?
- Is the popcorn at the bottom of a bag different from the popcorn at the top of the bag? If so, how is it different?

## Focus Question...
- How might we weigh popped popcorn?  What might affect the weight of popped popcorn?  Would temperature change the weight?  Humidity?

## Problem...
Last night Kwan made popcorn to eat while she watched a late-night television show.  There were just seven grams left over this morning to give to her friend Jonathan.  Estimate how many kernels of popped popcorn equal 7 grams, and mark your estimate on this chart.

### Kernels of Popcorn

| | |
|---|---|
| 1–50 | |
| 51–100 | |
| 101–150 | |
| 151–200 | |
| 201–300 | |
| 301–400 | |
| >400 | |

# KERNELS OF POPCORN

## Objectives
- to understand and apply ratios, proportions, and percents in a wide variety of situations
- to use estimation to check the reasonableness of results
- to extend students' understanding of the process of measurement

## Materials
Scales; 7 grams of weights (7 normal-sized paper clips will do); a large bag of popped popcorn; a box of plastic sandwich bags (NOTE: You will need to know how much an empty sandwich bag weighs, so weigh it before class.)

## Graphing
Have several students each choose one (1) kernel of popcorn. Record the number of kernels that weigh **over** or **under** one gram. Ask students to make inferences from the data gathered.

## Discussing
Pick four groups or students and give each person or group an empty plastic sandwich bag and a bowl of popped popcorn. Tell them that each group will have only three attempts to put 7 grams of popcorn in the bag. Ask each group to place what it thinks is the correct amount of popcorn into the bag and step forward to have it weighed. After each weighing, tell the group if their popcorn is "overweight" or "underweight," but don't tell them how far off they are.

If the class members work well together, they may wait for each group's results before the next group tries. This allows them to build their information upon the last response. But don't suggest this strategy. They should begin group cooperation on their own—if not by the second attempt, at least by the third and final time if you emphasize that "this is it—last try!")

If several groups are "right on" after three attempts of estimation, then have each count the kernels and average their results. If only one group is "right on," use that count. If no group is "right on," discuss how all groups might have changed their estimation procedures.

- They might have benefited from not taking out just a few each time but dividing the bag into two equal parts, increasing the odds of estimation.
- They might have utilized group cooperation.

Choose different groups and allow them three tries each at 7 grams of popcorn.

## Answering
Typically, 7 grams of popped corn will be from 1–50 kernels.

## Extending
- Does it make a difference if the popcorn is not popped?
- Change from popped popcorn to something lighter, like cereal.
- The game of "guess my number" can be played using the same principle. Which team or student can guess the number you are thinking of in the fewest guesses? State "too low" or "too high" after each guess.

# THE BASEBALL TOURNAMENT

### Initial Graph...
As a spectator at any baseball game, where would you prefer to sit? Mark your response on the chart below.

| | |
|---|---|
| **Behind Home Plate** | |
| **Behind First Base** | |
| **Behind Second Base** | |
| **Behind Third Base** | |

### Speaking of Baseball...
- When was the last time you went to a baseball game? How many innings did you see? How long did the game last?

- Have you ever been to a professional or college baseball game? Have you ever seen a professional or college baseball game on television? How do these differ from the baseball games you play on the school ground with your friends? Are professional games played any differently from Little League or Pony League games? If so, in what way?

- In what ways do teams try to make their baseball stadiums comfortable for spectators? Do they make any special provisions for handicapped spectators? If so, what? What else might they do to make the game and the ball park more enjoyable or accessible to handicapped persons?

### Focus Question...
- Have you ever been to a baseball tournament? How many teams were in the tournament? Did each team play every other team at least once? How was the winner determined?

### Problem...
Jennifer and Lamont didn't make the baseball team this year, but they always go watch the teams their friends play for.

Several of their friends' teams are playing in a tournament this week. If there are 5 baseball teams in this tournament, and if each team plays each of the other teams twice, how many games will be played altogether before the tournament ends?

# THE BASEBALL TOURNAMENT

## Objectives

- to generalize solutions and strategies to new problem situations
- to model situations using oral, written, concrete, graphical, and algebraic methods
- to make and evaluate mathematical conjectures and arguments
- to develop and use order relations for whole numbers, integers, and rational numbers

## Graphing

One approach might be to label the teams A, B, C, D, E and arrange combinations—such as AB indicating a game of team A against team B. One order of listing might be:

| AB | BC | CD | DE |
|----|----|----|----|
| AB | BC | CD | DE |
| AC | BD | CE |    |
| AC | BD | CE |    |
| AD | BE |    |    |
| AD | BE |    |    |
| AE |    |    |    |
| AE |    |    |    |

Or, using another grouping approach:

| AB | AC | AD | AE |
|----|----|----|----|
| BA | BC | BD | BE |
| CA | CB | CD | CE |
| DA | DB | DC | DE |
| EA | EB | EC | ED |

## Mathing

Students must get the idea that each pair of teams occurs twice. They might list them, taking them in order and beginning with team A: AB,AC,AD,AE—and A is done; it has been paired with every other team. Now, pair the second team (B) with each team that it has not already played: BC,BD,BE—and B is done. Proceed with the third team (C): CD,CE—and C is done. The fourth team (D) has been paired with all teams but one, so pair DE—and D is done. Team E has already been paired with all possible teams by the previous pairings. Have students count or add the number of pairs (games) necessary for each team to play every other team once (4 + 3 + 2 + 1 = 10 games). If each team had to play every other team twice, the the total number of games would be 2 × the original number, or 20.

## Discussing

Students should always have the opportunity of explaining how they chose their response and how they obtained the exact answer. Be sure to ask for other methods that may have been attempted in approaching this problem. You will be amazed at the varied responses.

## Answering

There would be 20 games in the tournament: 8 + 6 + 4 + 2 = 20 (or 5 × 4 = 20).

## Extending

What if a tournament with the same "round-robin" structure had 100 teams? Can you find a formula that would cover all cases?

| NUMBER OF TEAMS | GAMES |
|-----------------|-------|
| 2 | 2 |
| 3 | 6 |
| 4 | 12 |
| • | • |
| • | • |
| $n$ | $n(n-1)$ |

# PIGEONS AND CATS

### Initial Graph...

If two pigeons and one cat were sitting in a tree, they would have a total of:

|          | 1 head | 2 heads | 3 heads | 4 heads | 5 heads |
|----------|--------|---------|---------|---------|---------|
| 6 legs   |        |         |         |         |         |
| 8 legs   |        |         |         |         |         |
| 10 legs  |        |         |         |         |         |
| 12 legs  |        |         |         |         |         |
| 14 legs  |        |         |         |         |         |
| 16 legs  |        |         |         |         |         |

Mark your response on the matrix above.

---

### Speaking of Heads and Legs...

- Let's see if there is some way we can make a picture to help find the answer. First, let's consider heads. How many heads does each animal in the tree have? Draw a circle on scratch paper to represent a "head." Now draw enough lines extending out from the circle to show the number of legs on a pigeon. How many "legs" do you count?

- Now let's try using one circle to represent each animal's head. Draw a total of three circles on your scratch paper. If each animal was a pigeon, how many legs would each "head" have? How many total legs would the three animals have?

- Again, draw three circles as heads. Add legs as if one animal were a cat and the other two were pigeons. How many legs do they have total?

- Draw three circles again. Add legs as if two were cats and one a pigeon, and count the total.

- You have made a pattern by drawing three heads but taking away one pigeon and adding one cat each time. Can you predict what would come next in the pattern?

---

### Focus Question...

- We just made a pattern from a pattern. Do you think that making patterns would help solve larger problems that are similar?

---

### Problem...

José saw some pigeons and cats in the parking lot this morning. He counted 35 heads and 100 legs on these animals. Did he count more pigeons or more cats in the parking lot?

---

# PIGEONS AND CATS

## Objectives
- to acquire confidence in using mathematics meaningfully
- to model situations using oral, written, concrete, graphical, and algebraic methods
- to value the role of mathematics in our culture and society
- to develop number sense for whole numbers, integers, and rational numbers
- to develop, analyze, and explain computation procedures and estimation techniques
- to use patterns and functions to represent and solve problems
- to apply algebraic methods to solve a variety of real-world and mathematical problems

## Discussing
Did anyone attempt to find the exact number of pigeons and cats? Did anyone try to organize a system to cover different possibilities? For instance, the fact that 35 heads were counted indicates that the total number of creatures was 35. If there was 1 pigeon, there would be 34 cats. If 2 pigeons, 33 cats, and so on. Ask students to justify their answers. This is not the only method for solving the problem, and it is important to ask students to explain other methods they may have used.

## Graphing
In the following listing, the corresponding number of legs is shown in parenthesis.

| Pigeons | Cats | Total number |
|---------|------|--------------|
| 1 (2) | 34 (136) | 35 (138) |
| 2 (4) | 33 (132) | 35 (136) |
| 3 (6) | 32 (128) | 35 (134) |

## Mathing
Notice that a pattern develops with the total number of legs. As the number of pigeons increases by 1, the number of cats decreases by 1, and the total number of feet decreases by 2. Thus, for the total number of feet to be 100 the pattern would continue 17 more times, leaving the final number of pigeons at 20 and the final number of cats at 15. It is not necessary to extend the pattern all the way. It is more important to see the beginnings of the pattern in order to calculate where the desired result might be.

## Answering
20 pigeons + 15 cats = 35 heads
(2 legs × 20 pigeons) + (4 legs × 15 cats) = 40 + 60 = 100 legs

## Extending
- If a mixed group of rabbits and chickens totaled 50 creatures and 140 legs, how many of each animal would there be in the group? (Hint: If each chicken stood on one foot and each rabbit on two, the solution could be seen as needing only 70 legs.)

| Rabbits | Chickens | Legs | |
|---------|----------|------|--|
| 1 | 49 | 51 | |
| 2 | 48 | 52 | |
| 3 | 47 | 53 | a pattern can now |
| • | • | • | be noted, hence: |
| • | • | • | |
| • | • | • | |
| 20 | 30 | 70 | |

- Last year, the local cats caught 9,797 mice. If each cat caught an equal number of mice, and if every cat caught more mice than there were cats, then how many cats were involved and how many mice did each catch? (Since 9797 cannot be a prime number, it must have two unique factors. Encourage students to use their calculators to find them.)

# THREE-COURSE MEALS

## Initial Graph...

Choose your favorite meal combination from the given courses and mark it on the chart below.

|  | SOUP | OR | SALAD |
|---|---|---|---|
| CHICKEN |  |  |  |
| OR |  |  |  |
| BEEF |  |  |  |

## Speaking of Meals...

- How many different meals are possible from the choices given in the **Initial Graph** (above)? How did you figure it out?

- If we added one more type of meat to the choices above, how would the total number of possible meals be changed? How many different meat items would be needed to guarantee at least 15 different meals?

- Restaurants usually offer many choices of different meals. Why do you think they do this? What are the advantages and disadvantages of such a large number of choices?

## Focus Question...

- If the choice of soup or salad is considered the first course at a restaurant, and if the meat is considered the second course, what might be offered for the third course?

## Problem...

Courtney attends a boarding school and eats dinner in the school's cafeteria. If, for each dinner, she is allowed to choose only one item from each of the following courses, how many different meals can Courtney make?

| 1st course | soup or salad |
|---|---|
| 2nd course | chicken, beef, fish, or pork |
| 3rd course | ice cream, cake, or mousse |

# THREE-COURSE MEALS

## Objectives
- to explore problems and describe results using graphical, numerical, physical, algebraic, and verbal mathematical models or representations
- to understand, represent, and use numbers in a variety of equivalent forms in real-world and mathematical problem situations
- to describe, extend, analyze, and create a wide variety of patterns

## Discussing
Encourage students to develop a plan for symbolizing each item (unless, of course, they want to write out the complete name each time). One method might be to let letters represent specific food offerings:

| **First Course** | **Second Course** | **Third Course** |
|---|---|---|
| O = Soup | C = Chicken | I = Ice Cream |
| A = Salad | B = Beef | K = Cake |
| | F = Fish | M = Mousse |
| | P = Pork | |

In abbreviated form, then, the listing would appear:

| 1st course | O  A |
|---|---|
| 2nd course | C  B  F  P |
| 3rd course | I  K  M |

Listen carefully to alternative methods that students may have of justifying their answers.

## Graphing
A combination for a meal might now be represented by OCI: representing *soup, chicken,* and *ice cream.* An organized listing can then be formed of all such meals:

| OCI | OCK | OCM | ACI | ACK | ACM |
|---|---|---|---|---|---|
| OBI | OBK | OBM | ABI | ABK | ABM |
| OFI | OFK | OFM | AFI | AFK | AFM |
| OPI | OPK | OPM | API | APK | APM |

## Mathing
Each first course choice will match with four second course choices ($2 \times 4 = 8$). Each of these 8 pairs will then match with three third-course items ($8 \times 3 = 24$).

## Answering
There are 24 different possible meals given the choices of the above three courses: 2 (first course choices) × 4 (second course choices) × 3 (third course choices) = 24 meals

## Extending
Suppose that you wanted to buy a new car. In the process of looking, you find that, for the car you want, there are 10 color options, 6 engine options, 5 transmissions options, 9 light packages, 9 wheel options, 5 audio options, 8 tire options, and 7 interior options. (Nothing is simple in this world anymore.) How many cars would have to be built before two identical cars had to occur?

# COMPARATIVE AGES

**Initial Graph...**
Find and color in the square on the graph that shows how old you are today **and** how old you will be six years from now.

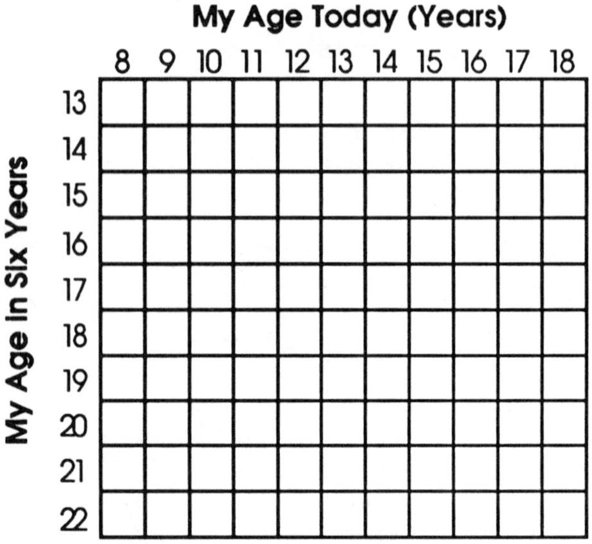

**My Age Today (Years)**

|  | 8 | 9 | 10 | 11 | 12 | 13 | 14 | 15 | 16 | 17 | 18 |
|---|---|---|---|---|---|---|---|---|---|---|---|
| 13 |  |  |  |  |  |  |  |  |  |  |  |
| 14 |  |  |  |  |  |  |  |  |  |  |  |
| 15 |  |  |  |  |  |  |  |  |  |  |  |
| 16 |  |  |  |  |  |  |  |  |  |  |  |
| 17 |  |  |  |  |  |  |  |  |  |  |  |
| 18 |  |  |  |  |  |  |  |  |  |  |  |
| 19 |  |  |  |  |  |  |  |  |  |  |  |
| 20 |  |  |  |  |  |  |  |  |  |  |  |
| 21 |  |  |  |  |  |  |  |  |  |  |  |
| 22 |  |  |  |  |  |  |  |  |  |  |  |

**My Age In Six Years**

**Speaking of Ages...**
- Do you have a brother or sister whose age would fit on this graph? Where would his or her response be marked?
- Look at the extremes. What is the current age of the youngest person whose age could be marked on the graph above? Where would his or her response be? What is the current age of the oldest person whose age could be marked on the graph? Where would his or her response be marked?
- What do all the marked responses have in common?

**Focus Question...**
- If you had a friend and if you were twice as old as that friend, what age would your friend be? If you were three times as old as your friend, then what age would your friend be?
- Are there certain ages that cannot be exactly two or three times another person's age? Name some of them.

**Problem...**
Today, Ralph is three times as old as Concha. Six years from now, Ralph will be twice as old as Concha. How old is Ralph right now?

# COMPARATIVE AGES

## Objectives
- to model situations using oral, written, concrete, graphical, and algebraic methods
- to represent numerical relationships in one- and two-dimensional graphs
- to use estimation to check the reasonableness of results
- to use patterns and functions to represent and solve problems
- to develop confidence in solving linear equations using concrete, informal, and formal methods

## Graphing
Ask students to explain the method they used to arrive at their solution. Perhaps some assumed that Concha was one year old and proceeded to build a chart of possible ages for Concha and Ralph.

| Concha's age | 1 | 2 | 3 | 4 | 5 | 6 | 7 | 8 | 9••• |
|---|---|---|---|---|---|---|---|---|---|
| Ralph's age | 3 | 6 | 9 | 12 | 15 | 18 | 21 | 24 | 27••• |

A record of their ages in six years can then be placed below this chart for comparison.

| Concha's age | 1 | 2 | 3 | 4 | 5 | 6 | 7 | 8 | 9••• |
|---|---|---|---|---|---|---|---|---|---|
| Ralph's age | 3 | 6 | 9 | 12 | 15 | 18 | 21 | 24 | 27••• |
| Concha's age in 6 years | 7 | 8 | 9 | 10 | 11 | 12 | 13 | 14 | 15••• |
| Ralph's age in 6 years | 9 | 12 | 15 | 18 | 21 | 24 | 27 | 30 | 36••• |

From this information it is possible to see that when Concha is 12 Ralph will be twice her age. That makes Ralph 18 and Concha 6 at the present time.

## Mathing
Help the students construct the graph step by step, one row at a time. For example, Concha's age goes up 1 for each cell. Ralph's age is 3 times Concha's age at the present time, so his row is the result of multiplying the age in each of Concha's cells by 3. Concha's age in six years adds 6 to each of her cells, and the same for Ralph. This process results in the graph shown.

## Discussing
If students had worked only the first two or three ages in the chart above, could they have then known enough about the pattern to find the correct answer to the problem? Even more important than arriving at the correct answer is the way students justify how they arrived at Ralph's current age.

## Answering
Ralph is 18 years old.

## Extending
- Could this problem be solved in terms of an algebraic equation? [$3x + 6 = 2(x + 6)$]
- If Ralph is five times as old as Concha is today, and if all other conditions remain the same, how old is Ralph now?

# A NUMBER FOR 48

**Initial Graph...**
Write your favorite number on the line below.

_____

**Speaking of Numbers...**
- If you add three to your favorite number, what is your result? How could you find your favorite number if you only knew the sum of that number and three?
- Now, take your favorite number, add three, and multiply the sum by seven. What is your final answer? How could you find your favorite number from that final answer?

_____

**Focus Question...**
- Define two mathematical rules that can be performed in sequence with any favorite number. Write those two rules down, then write the final answer from applying those two rules to your favorite number. Share the final answer and the rules with a friend. Ask them to find your beginning (favorite) number.

_____

**Problem...**
Lorenzo asked Fritz to pick a number, add 3 to it, multiply that sum by 7, then subtract 11 and double the result. Fritz did what Lorenzo asked and said that his final answer was 48.

Without hesitation, Lorenzo said he knew what number Fritz had used to begin! What number do you think Fritz started with to get an answer of 48? Write your response on the graph below.

| Final Number | Beginning Number |
|:---:|:---:|
| 48 | |

# A NUMBER FOR 48

## Objectives
- to extend the understanding of whole-number operations to fractions, decimals, integers, and rational numbers
- to use estimation to check the reasonableness of results
- to represent situations and number patterns with tables, graphs, verbal rules, and equations and to explore the interrelationships of these representations

## Mathing
Some students will justify their answer by starting with different numbers, like 1 (which doesn't work), then 2 (which does work). Generally, someone will want to start with the final answer of 48 and work backward. Each operation would then be the opposite. The opposite of *double* would be *divide by two*. The opposite of *subtracting* 11 would be *adding* 11. The opposite of *multiplying* by 7 would be *dividing* by 7. The opposite of *adding* 3 would be *subtracting* 3. Writing this out, the backward solution would be:

$$48 \div 2 = 24 \quad \text{(opposite of double)}$$
$$24 + 11 = 35 \quad \text{(opposite of subtracting 11)}$$
$$35 \div 7 = 5 \quad \text{(opposite of multiplying by 7)}$$
$$5 - 3 = 2 \quad \text{(opposite of adding 3)}$$

## Graphing
The process may be graphically represented with a line or bar graph similar to the one shown here.

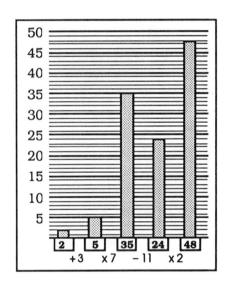

## Discussing
It is important to ask if anyone used a different method in approaching this problem. Ask students to demonstrate how they worked it, explaining each step they took and why.

## Answering
The beginning number was 2.

$$2 + 3 = 5$$
$$5 \times 7 = 35$$
$$35 - 11 = 24$$
$$24 \times 2 = 48$$

## Extending
- Try to find other combinations that work. What if you subtracted 10 instead of 11? Would the result then be a fraction?
- Suppose Fritz chose a number, added 3.5, multiplied this sum by 2.5, then subtracted 1.5, and doubled the result for a final answer of 19.5. What number had he started with this time?

## ACROSS THE UNITED STATES

**Initial Graph...**
If you were to travel across the United States, which area of this diagram shows the means of transportation you would prefer for the trip?

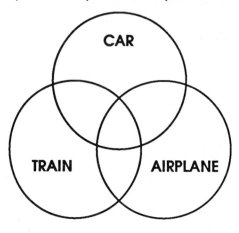

**Speaking of Travel...**
- What advantages might each type of transportation in the **Initial Graph** have over each of the other? What disadvantages might each have?

- Suppose you were traveling by car across the United States. What cities would you travel between? Find a route to take and show it on a map. Figure out approximately how many miles your trip would be.

- How many different routes can you find to get from San Francisco to New York City? Which route do you think has the shortest travel time? Which route has the longest distance?

- Try to find two cities in the United States where the shortest travel distance between them is greater than the shortest travel distance between San Francisco and New York. Name the two cities you chose.

- For a trip across the United States, would a car, a train, or an airplane cost you the most total trip money? What expenses might you have for each?

**Focus Question...**
- How many tires does the average person have available on a long car trip? Do most cars have spare tires? How many? What might you do to keep the tire wear balanced on a car trip across the United States?

**Problem...**
Miriam decided to take an automobile trip of 4000 miles across the United States. She rotated her tires (the four that were on the car and the one spare) so that at the end of the trip each tire had been used for the same number of miles. How many miles had been driven on each tire?

# ACROSS THE UNITED STATES

## Objectives
- to acquire confidence in using mathematics meaningfully
- to value the role of mathematics in our culture and society
- to understand and apply ratios, proportions, and percents in a variety of situations
- to use computation, estimation, and proportions to solve problems

## Graphing
The problem might be graphically represented using a line of set length.

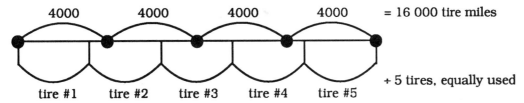

4000          4000          4000          4000          = 16 000 tire miles

tire #1      tire #2      tire #3      tire #4      tire #5          + 5 tires, equally used

## Mathing
Since there are 4 tires turning at one time for 4000 miles, 16 000 total miles are covered by all the tires. Miriam, however, used 5 tires to cover the 16 000 miles, so 16 000 ÷ 5 = 3200 miles covered by each tire.

## Discussing
Ask students to justify their answers. Many will assume that since there are four tires running on the car at a time, a 4000-mile trip put 4000 miles on each tire. But that response does not allow for the spare-tire factor. And 4000 ÷ 5 could not be the correct response either, as that would not allow for the fact that there are 4 wheels turning at any one time on the car. Another approach is needed.

## Answering
Each of the five tires had been driven for 3200 miles.

## Extending
- Suppose that Miriam extended her trip to 5000 miles and rotated not one, but two, spare tires so that at the end of her trip each of the six tires had been used for the same number of miles. How many miles would have been driven on each tire now?
- Make a two-dimensional graph showing the number of miles per tire compared to the total number of miles for the trip. Leave the variable of the number of tires constant at 5, but change the length of the trip.

# DAISY PETALS

**Initial Graph...**
Mark the area of the diagram that shows your personal response.

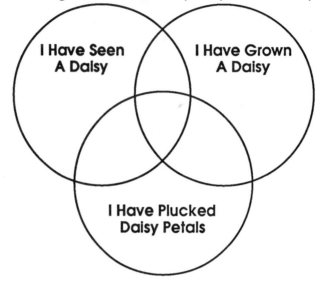

**I Have Seen A Daisy**

**I Have Grown A Daisy**

**I Have Plucked Daisy Petals**

**Speaking of Daisies...**
- What does a daisy look like? Can you draw a picture of one? What color(s) can they be?
- What conditions are necessary for a daisy to grow? What time of year would you plant one? Who could you ask for information on planting?
- In what parts of the world do daisies grow? How can you find out?

**Focus Question...**
- Do all daisies have the same number of petals?
- Is plucking flower petals a tradition in certain countries? If so, which ones? Locate those countries on a map.
- Have you ever heard of anyone "picking petals from a daisy"? Why would they want to do that? Do they follow any pattern in plucking the petals? If so, what is it?

**Problem...**
Perry found a large daisy with many petals—15 petals to be exact. Starting with petal number 1 and going in a clockwise order, he plucked every other petal until only one petal remained. If the first petal plucked was petal number 2, which petal number was the last one plucked?

# DAISY PETALS

## Objectives
- to develop and apply number-theory concepts (e.g., primes, factors, multiples) in real-world and mathematical problem situations
- to describe, extend, analyze, and create a wide variety of patterns
- to analyze tables and graphs to identify properties and relationships

## Discussing
A model works very effectively for plucking. Mark an X on each plucked petal until it can finally be demonstrated which petal remains. This isn't such a great math problem—unless it is extended as shown below.

## Answering
Demonstration shows that number 15 is the last remaining petal.

## Extending
What if there had been 100 petals on this daisy? Then which petal would remain?

## Graphing
One way for students to organize their thoughts on this problem might be to graph a chart showing which petal is left on daisies with varying numbers of petals. Students should soon recognize that petal 1 is left several times. Rewriting these facts and beginning a new group each time "petal 1" is encountered leads to the following chart.

| # of petals to start | petal # remaining | # of petals to start | petal # remaining | # of petals to start | petal # remaining |
|:---:|:---:|:---:|:---:|:---:|:---:|
| 1 | 1 | 8 | 1 | 16 | 1 |
|   |   | 9 | 3 | 17 | 3 |
| 2 | 1 | 10 | 5 | 18 | 5 |
| 3 | 3 | 11 | 7 | 19 | 7 |
|   |   | 12 | 9 | 20 | 9 |
| 4 | 1 | 13 | 11 | 21 | 11 |
| 5 | 3 | 14 | 13 | 22 | 13 |
| 6 | 5 | 15 | 15 | 23 | 15 |
| 7 | 7 |   |   | 24 | 17 |
|   |   |   |   | 25 | 19 |
|   |   |   |   | 26 | 21 |
|   |   |   |   | 27 | 23 |
|   |   |   |   | 28 | 25 |
|   |   |   |   | 29 | 27 |
|   |   |   |   | 30 | 29 |
|   |   |   |   | 31 | 31 |

Notice that the first group contains the first odd number. The second group contains the first two consecutive odd numbers, the third the first four consecutive odd numbers, the next the first eight, the next the first sixteen, and so on.

## Mathing
At this point a pattern forms, with each successive group doubling the number of consecutive odd numbers. Further development generates a formula for the number of the last remaining petal to be equal to $2(x - 2y) + 1$, where $x$ = the number of petals and $y$ = the greatest power of 2 less than or equal to $x$.

# WHAT ALFRED LIKES

**Initial Graph...**
Choose one of the following numbers and mark an X through it.

**16**          **44**

---

**Speaking of Numbers...**
- Can you think of anything that 16 and 44 have in common?
- What qualities does one number have that the other does not have? List other numbers that share these same qualities.
- Think of some times that people get a chance to choose a favorite number (lotto, telephone numbers, etc.).
- Can "favorite numbers" be random? Why or why not?
- Are there certain numbers that have been popular for hundred of years? What are they? Why do you think they are popular? Are certain numbers disliked? What are they and why do you think they are disliked?
- Do popular and unpopular numbers change according to time? (Do they get more or less popular over the years?) Do they change for different cultures or different countries?

---

**Problem...**
Alfred has some definite likes and dislikes when it comes to numbers.

He likes these.          He does not like these.

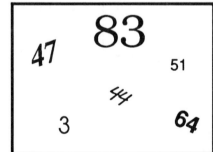

Which of the following numbers do you think he would like? Put an **X** in the column under each of your choices.

| 86 | 25 | 72 | 40 | 64 | 100 |
|----|----|----|----|----|-----|
|    |    |    |    |    |     |

 © 1990 Midwest Publications • Critical Thinking Press & Software, P.O. Box 448, Pacific Grove, CA 93950

# WHAT ALFRED LIKES

### Objectives
- to understand how the basic arithmetic operations are related to one another
- to develop and apply number-theory concepts (e.g., primes, factors, multiples) in real-world and mathematical problem situations

### Discussing
This is one of our favorite problems. The challenge comes in keeping overanxious students from blurting out the answer long enough to allow some thinking time for others.

Approach the problem by asking students to think of a number, then quickly tell them whether or not Alfred likes that number. Open-minded students who do not immediately see that Alfred likes the square of integers may find different ways of determining what it is he does or does not like.

### Graphing
We had one student who would not give up. While others realized that 49 = 7 × 7 and 1 = 1 × 1 and 9 = 3 × 3 and so on, she insisted upon a method of putting order to what Alfred liked and did not like.

| He liked (in order) | He did not like (in consecutive order) |
|---|---|
| 1 | 2, 3 |
| 4 | 5, 6, 7, 8 |
| 9 | 10, 11, 12, 13, 14, 15 |
| 16 | 17, 18, 19, 20, 21, 22, 23, 24 |
| 25 | 26, 27, 28, 29, 30, 31, 32, 33, 34, 35 |
| 36 | 37, 38, ••• |

This student discovered, by placing the integers in consecutive order, that Alfred liked the first integer, didn't like the next two integers, liked the next, didn't like the next four integers, liked the next, didn't like six integers, and so on—each time increasing the number of integers "not liked" by two. It was not only a good experience for her to discover on her own a method of justifying her response, but for other students as well to realize that there is more than one way to solve the same problem.

### Answering
Alfred likes numbers that are the square of integers, so he would like 25 (5 × 5), 64 (8 × 8), and 100 (10 × 10).

### Extending
- Make up similar problems by determining a relationship, writing down five or six numbers "liked" and "disliked," and respond to the class's guesses until the group sees the relationship.
- Play this game with relationships other than numbers, say with shapes or letters (combined curved and straight-line shapes, vowels, certain letters, number of letters, groupings or types, etc.).

## COUNTING BY 3, BY 4, AND BY 5

**Initial Graph...**
Write the next three numbers in the sequence if you were counting by 3s.

<u>3</u>   <u>6</u>   <u>9</u>   <u>12</u>   <u>  </u>   <u>  </u>   <u>  </u>

**Speaking of Counting...**
- What number did we start with to count by 3s? Will it end?
- If you were delivering 30 newspapers and put a special flier in every third one, how many fliers would you need? What if you needed to put an advertisement in every fourth newspaper? How many advertisements would you need?
- If these 30 newspapers were piled in numerical order, what number(s) would have both a flier **and** an advertisement in them?

**Focus Question...**
- If thirty people stood in the front of the room and counted off in numerical order, and if every third person put his or her right hand up, and if every fourth person put his or her left hand up, what people would have both hands up?
- If we continued the line of people, what would the numbers be of those people who held up both hands? Make a list of those numbers. What do the numbers on the list have in common?

**Problem...**
Peggy wants to know if there is any common number less than 100 that is used when we count by 3s, by 4s, and by 5s. If there is such a number, help her find it. What kind of graph could use to show how you got your answer?

# COUNTING BY 3, BY 4, AND BY 5

## Objectives

- to develop and apply a variety of strategies to solve problems, with emphasis on multistep and nonroutine problems
- to develop and use order relations for whole numbers, integers, and rational numbers
- to develop and apply number-theory concepts (e.g., primes, factors, multiples) in real-world and mathematical problem situations
- to describe and represent relationships with tables, graphs, and rules

## Graphing

A pattern is made by "highlight counting," using circles for 3s, squares for 4s, and triangles for 5s (as shown to the right). The first number with all three symbols is the lowest common multiple.

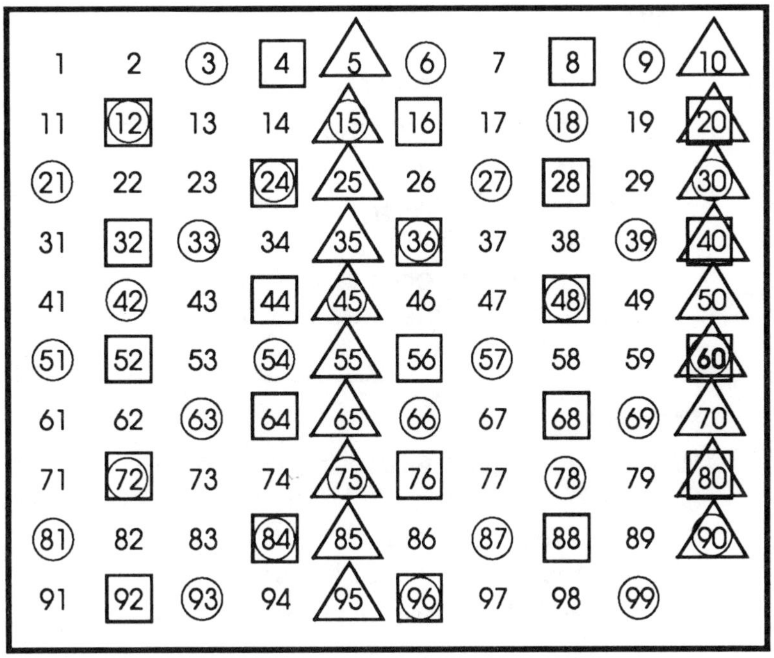

## Discussing

Ask students to explain how they approached this problem. Did they start with the 3s and work up? Did they begin with the largest number (5) and multiply it over and over until the proper number was found? Some students will see immediately that $3 \times 4 \times 5 = 60$, the number they were looking for. But what if some numbers had common factors of others? They should soon realize that what they are looking for is the *least common multiple* of the numbers.

## Answering

The number Peggy was looking for is 60.

## Extending

- What is the smallest number used when we count by **all even positive digits** (2, 4, 6, 8, 10, •••)?
- What is the smallest number used when we count by $3x + 6$ and $4x + 8$, where $x$ represents a counting number?

# FIGURING YOUR BIRTH DAY

**Initial Graph...**
On what day of the week do you think you were born? Mark your answer on the graph below.

| Mon. | Tues. | Wed. | Thur. | Fri. | Sat. | Sun. |
|------|-------|------|-------|------|------|------|
|      |       |      |       |      |      |      |

**Speaking of Day of Birth...**
- If you do not know on which day of the week your were born, where could you go to find that information?
- Are there certain days of the week that have a higher birth rate than others? Using the local newspaper, keep track of the total number of births on each day for one week in the local hospital(s). Which day had the greatest number of births?
- How many people in this room do you think may have been born on the same day of the week as you?

**Problem...**
Walker wondered what day of the week he was born. Was he born on Sunday? On Tuesday? Hillary said he could find out if he'd follow these steps.

**Add these four numbers:**
1. The last two digits of the year he was born.
2. The quotient (but not remainder) of dividing the last two digits of the year he was born by four.
3. The number for the month he was born, taken from this list:

| January............1 (0 if leap year) | July ......................................0 |
|---|---|
| February.........4 (3 if leap year) | August................................3 |
| March...............4 | September......................6 |
| April....................0 | October.............................1 |
| May...................2 | November.......................4 |
| June.................5 | December........................6 |

4. The day of the month he was born.

**Divide the sum by seven. The remainder will tell which day of the week he was born:**

| Remainder | Day of birth | Remainder | Day of birth |
|---|---|---|---|
| 0.........................Saturday | | 4....................Wednesday |
| 1............................ Sunday | | 5........................... Thursday |
| 2......................... Monday | | 6..............................Friday |
| 3............................Tuesday | | |

Walker was born January 24, 1975. So he added:

$$75 + 18 + 1 + 24 = 118.$$

He found that dividing this sum (118) by seven gave him a remainder of 6. Walker was born on Friday! On what day of the week were you born?

# FIGURING YOUR BIRTH DAY

## Objectives
- to acquire confidence in using mathematics meaningfully
- to appreciate the value of mathematical notation and its role in the development of mathematical ideas
- to appreciate the use and power of reasoning as a part of mathematics
- to value the role of mathematics in our culture and society
- to develop and apply number-theory concepts (e.g., primes, factors, multiples) in real-world and mathematical problem situations

## Discussing
Ask students to demonstrate the steps they performed to find the day of the week on which they were born. (I was shocked one time to have a student look it up in the phone book, but hopefully your first demonstration will follow the mathematical steps outlined in the problem.)

- Why did students need to consider leap years if they were born in January or February?
- How does one find a leap year anyway? (Walker knew the year of his birth wasn't a leap year because it wasn't divisible by four and didn't end in 00.)

## Graphing
After the demonstration—and when their work has been checked—have students record their birth "days" on a class graph and consider the results. *"Did any day of the week have the majority (one more than half the total) of births? Which day(s) had a plurality (more than any other day)? Could there be a reason for this? Do hospitals report more births on certain days?"*

## Answering
The answer will vary with individuals.

## Extending
- On what day of the week were other members of your family members born? Are there any duplicates?
- On what day of the week did Christopher Columbus first land in America?
- What day of the week was the first day of the twentieth century? (Be careful; the first day of the twentieth century was January 1, 1901, not 1900. Can you explain why?)
- Walker, who enjoys history, was wondering when the majority of United States' wars have been proclaimed. Certainly they must not have been proclaimed on a weekend, as Congress would not be in session. Perhaps politicians discuss situations over the weekends and then jump into action on Monday. Can you find if there has been any pattern or most-common day for declaration of war by the United States?

# SQUASH

### Initial Graph...
How do you like squash fixed?  Do you like it baked in a pie?  In bread?  Cut up in a salad?  Mark the area of the diagram below to show your choice.

**I Like Squash In:**

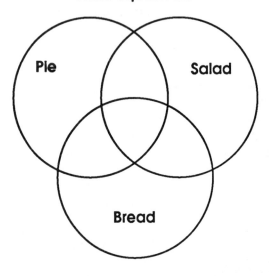

### Speaking of Squash...
- Name some ways of fixing squash that are not shown in the **Initial Graph**.
- There are several different types of squash.  Name some.  Can they all be eaten?  Do they all taste alike?  Are certain kinds better for certain dishes?
- Are squash easy to grow in our area?  If so, which types of squash are most commonly grown?
- In what countries would you expect squash to grow?  In what countries would you expect squash to be impossible to grow?  In what country did squash originate?
- What type of food value does squash have?  How can you find out?

### Focus Question...
- There is a squash on my desk. What type is it?  What food dishes could we prepare from it?  How much do you think it weighs?

### Problem...
Fumiko wants to make a salad for the picnic this weekend, and she decided to buy some squash to put in it.  She chose the one on the desk and paid 86 cents for it.  How much **per pound** do you think she paid for this squash?

# SQUASH

## Objectives
- to estimate, make, and use measurements to describe and compare phenomena
- to construct, read, and interpret tables, charts, and graphs
- to develop, analyze, and explain computation procedures and estimation techniques

## Materials
A summer squash (like one might put in a salad) and a scale suitable for weighing it (also an orange and a sack of potatoes for the **Extending** activities)

## Discussing
Ask students to justify their responses and to explain the processes they used in arriving at an estimate and at a final solution. *"How did you try to determine the weight of the squash for your estimate? Is weight the first data necessary to solve this problem? How will you weigh the squash? How accurate does this weighing have to be? Should it be to the closest pound? The closest half-pound? The closest ounce? Once you have found the weight, what then?* (Hopefully some will try dividing the total amount (86¢) by the weight. Ask them to explain why.) *Are there other ways to arrive at a solution?"*

## Mathing
If a one-pound squash cost 86 cents, what would a two-pound squash cost? What about a 2.5-pound squash?

## Graphing
Can you show the information from the **Mathing** section on a graph? Can you tell the cost of a squash of any weight by extending the graph? If you know how much it cost, can you use the graph to tell the weight of any squash that costs 86¢ a pound?

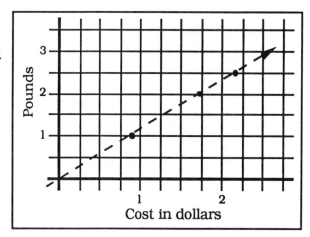

## Answering
The price per pound depends upon the weight of the squash.

## Extending
- My grocery bill this morning was $1.68 for this orange and one head of lettuce. If the lettuce was 69¢ a head, what did they charge me per pound for the orange?
- The sign over the potatoes I bought at the grocery store yesterday said they cost 50¢ per pound. How much do you think I had to pay for these potatoes?

# COST OF A WATERMELON

**Initial Graph...**
How well do you like to eat watermelon?  Mark your response by checking the box of your choice.

☐ **I Like Watermelon**  ☐ **I Do Not Like Watermelon**
☐ **I Have Never Tasted Watermelon**

---

**Speaking of Watermelon...**
- What kind of plant does a watermelon grow on?  Do the melons grow better in hot or cool climates?  Can we grow watermelons here?
- Where did watermelons first grow?  Where and when was their first recorded appearance in North America?  What states grow the most watermelons now?
- Why do you think they are called "watermelons"?

---

**Focus Question...**
- How much do you think an average watermelon weighs?  See if you can find out the "record" weights, both smallest and largest, for a watermelon.

---

**Problem...**
Yoshio paid 69¢ a pound for the watermelon on the desk.  How much do you think the melon cost him?

| | | | | | |
|---|---|---|---|---|---|
| .01–.20 | | 1.01–1.20 | | 2.01–2.20 | |
| .21–.40 | | 1.21–1.40 | | 2.21–2.40 | |
| .41–.60 | | 1.41–1.60 | | 2.41–2.60 | |
| .61–.80 | | 1.61–1.80 | | 2.61–2.80 | |
| .81–1.00 | | 1.81–2.00 | | 2.81–3.00 | |
| | | | | | |
| 3.01–3.20 | | 4.01–4.20 | | 5.01–5.20 | |
| 3.21–3.40 | | 4.21–4.40 | | 5.21–5.40 | |
| 3.41–3.60 | | 4.41–4.60 | | 5.41–5.60 | |
| 3.61–3.80 | | 4.61–4.80 | | 5.61–5.80 | |
| 3.81–4.00 | | 4.81–5.00 | | > 5.81 | |

# COST OF A WATERMELON

## Objectives
- to construct, read, and interpret tables, charts, and graphs
- to understand the structure and use of systems of measurement
- to compute with whole numbers, decimals, integers, and rational numbers
- to understand and appreciate the need for numbers beyond the whole numbers

## Materials
A watermelon and a scales

## Graphing
Ask students what the watermelon would cost if it weighed one pound, two pounds, three pounds, and so on. Help them use this information to graph a chart.

| weight of melon | 1 lb. | 2 lb. | 3 lb. | 4 lb. | 5 lb. | 6 lb. | 7 lb. | 8 lb. |
|---|---|---|---|---|---|---|---|---|
| price of melon | 69¢ | $1.38 | $2.07 | $2.76 | $3.45 | $4.14 | $4.83 | $5.52 |

This will also help them visualize parts of pounds and estimate costs. (If a watermelon weighs between 1 and 2 pounds, the price must be between 69¢ and $1.38, and so on.)

## Mathing
Weigh the watermelon to the nearest tenth of a pound. Now, focus again on the chart above. If the watermelon weighed four pounds, a method of obtaining the cost ($2.76) was to multiply $.69 by 4; for the cost of a six-pound watermelon, multiply $.69 by 6.

Another way of finding the watermelon's cost is to realize that each tenth of a pound costs 6.9¢. For example, if the watermelon weighs 2.2 pounds, then its cost would be:

$$\begin{aligned} &\$1.380 \text{ for two pounds} \\ &\phantom{\$1}.069 \text{ for one-tenth a pound} \\ + &\phantom{\$1}\underline{.069} \text{ for one-tenth a pound} \\ &\$1.518 \quad \text{(or } \$1.52 \text{ rounded)} \end{aligned}$$

## Answering
The cost of the watermelon is found by multiplying its weight by .69 (69 cents).

## Extending
- Would a two-dimensional graph of cost versus weight help more quickly determine the cost of any watermelon? Extend the following graph and find out.

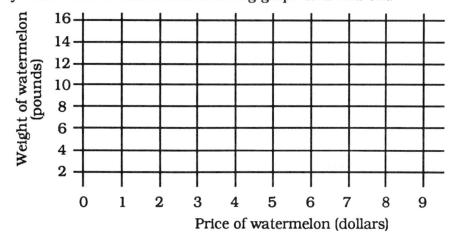

- How much of a watermelon's weight is water? Try some experiments to help you make an estimate. Put your answer in decimal form.

# YOUR HEIGHT IN PENNIES

**Problem...**

A friend of mine once said that anyone who could estimate the value of his or her height in stacked pennies could keep the pennies. She says that she has never had to give away any pennies.

Do you think you could do it? Let's have a contest. Estimate the value (in dollars and cents) of a stack of pennies as tall as you are, and put your name beside your estimate.

| Estimate | Name |
|---|---|
| $ . | |
| $ . | |
| $ . | |
| $ . | |
| $ . | |
| $ . | |
| $ . | |
| $ . | |
| $ . | |
| $ . | |
| $ . | |
| $ . | |
| $ . | |
| $ . | |
| $ . | |
| $ . | |
| $ . | |
| $ . | |
| $ . | |
| $ . | |
| $ . | |
| $ . | |
| $ . | |
| $ . | |
| $ . | |

# YOUR HEIGHT IN PENNIES

## Objectives
- to generalize solutions and strategies to new problem situations
- to validate personal thinking
- to use a mathematical idea to further understanding of other mathematical ideas
- to use estimation to check the reasonableness of results
- to develop, analyze, and explain computation procedures and estimation techniques

## Materials
Meter stick or yard stick (for measuring height), 5–10 rulers, and 50–100 pennies

## Discussing
Before students attempt to solve the problem, ask each student to place his or her height without shoes (either known or measured against a wall) beside their name. Divide the class into groups and give each group a small ruler and 10 pennies. Ask students to use these materials to establish the value of each person's height in stacked pennies and to write that value beside the estimate. Encourage them to discuss any problems they encountered when estimating a height in such small units.

(We have given this problem to several classes and have never had anyone estimate the exact value of his or her height. You may wish to give a sticker or some other small reward to the student whose estimate came closest to his or her actual height value.)

## Mathing
When the last group has finished, ask each group to explain the method they used to find the value of stacked pennies. One group may find 8 pennies totals ½ inch and figure 16 pennies to each full inch. The values of an individual's height would then be found by multiplying 16 cents by the correct number of inches. Other groups may use other methods, such as using all the pennies given or using one penny only.

## Graphing
Have students make a chart like the one shown below comparing the value of various heights in stacked pennies. Ask them if they could use any other type of graph to show this comparison. Have them demonstrate and justify their choices.

| Height | 4'10" | 4'11" | 5' | 5'1" | 5'2" | 5'3" | 5'4" | 5'5" | 5'6" | 5'7" | 5'8" |
|---|---|---|---|---|---|---|---|---|---|---|---|
| Inches | 58" | 59" | 60" | 61" | 62" | 63" | 64" | 65" | 66" | 67" | 68" |
| $ Value | 9.28 | 9.44 | 9.60 | 9.76 | 9.92 | 10.08 | 10.24 | 10.40 | 10.56 | 10.72 | 10.88 |

## Answering
There are 16 pennies to the inch.

## Extending
- Would the value of your height in stacked nickels be five times the value of your height in stacked pennies? Estimate the value of your height in nickels, then find the real value.
- Find the difference in value between your height in dimes and your height in quarters.

# HOW LONG WILL IT TAKE TO BUY A RADIO?

**Initial Graph...**
Why do you listen to the radio? Color the area on the diagram below that most accurately shows your reason or reasons.

**Speaking of Radios...**
- How many radios do you have in your home? Are they all the same or are they different kinds? How many different kinds of radios can you think of that people might own?
- Is there a particular time of the day when you usually listen to the radio? Why do you listen at that time more than at any other?
- How long has the radio been around? Who invented the radio? What famous radio broadcasts have you heard? What famous radio broadcasts have you heard your parents or grandparents talk about?
- How has the invention of the radio affected modern civilization? Are there still countries or places where radios are not common?

**Focus Question...**
- If you wanted to buy a portable radio (battery operated) today, how much do you think you would have to pay for it?

**Problem...**
Rey gets a weekly allowance of $1.75. He also mows a neighbor's lawn for $3.50 a week. Another neighbor has recently asked him to mow her lawn also for $3.50 a week. Everyone pays him on Friday only. So far, Rey has saved $9.35.

He would like to buy a radio that costs $45.99. If he saves all the money from his allowance and his jobs, how many weeks will it take him to save enough money to buy that radio?

# HOW LONG WILL IT TAKE TO BUY A RADIO?

## Objectives
- to evaluate arguments that are based on data analysis
- to investigate relationships among fractions, decimals, and percents
- to understand, represent, and use numbers in a variety of equivalent forms (integer, decimal, percent) in real-world and mathematical problem situations

## Graphing
There are several methods of showing this problem graphically. One possibility is to use a number line to represent the savings goal. Have students justify their rationale for choosing the graph they used.

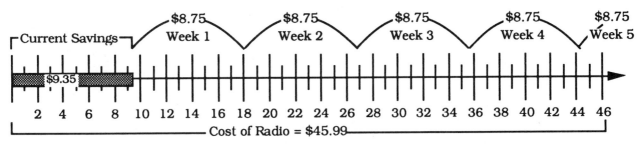

## Mathing
One method is to begin with the $45.99 and reduce:

| | |
|---|---|
| $45.99 | cost of radio |
| − 9.35 | saved so far |
| $36.64 | Amount remaining |

then figure the weekly income:

| | |
|---|---|
| $1.75 | allowance |
| 3.50 | one lawn job |
| 3.50 | second lawn job |
| $8.75 | earned each week |

and divide to find the result:

$$\frac{\$36.64 \text{ (amount needed)}}{\$8.75 \text{ (earned each week)}} = 4.2 \text{ weeks, which must be rounded up to 5 weeks.}$$

## Discussing
Ask the students to justify their answers. If they wonder why it is necessary to round up, remind them Rey is paid for his work only on Friday, not at midweek, and that the entire week must be worked for the amount needed for a fraction of a week. (Besides, Rey might use the extra money to buy batteries.)

Ask for other methods. Some students may have estimated the amount earned per week, then subtracted from the total amount for the radio (week by week) until $9.35 was left.

## Answering
Rey needs to work 5 weeks to have enough money to guarantee purchasing the radio.

## Extending
What if Rey's current weekly allowance of $23.50 increases by one dollar. He has two jobs, one which pays $13.22 per week and the other, a daily newspaper delivery, pays him $5.00 per day. If he has no money saved so far, and if he saves all the money he gets, how many weeks will it take him to save the money for a $45.99 radio and an $80 graphics calculator?

# HOW MUCH FOR CANDY BARS FOR EVERYONE?

**Initial Graph...**
Put a mark under the first letter in the name of your favorite candy bar.

A B C D E F G H I J K L M N O P Q R S T U V W X Y Z

---

**Speaking of Candy Bars...**
- What candy bar do you think is the class favorite? What are the top three favorites? Would these still be the top three if you surveyed every student in school?
- Are more candy bars eaten by younger or older people? Why? Does the average person eat more candy in the winter than in the summer? Why or why not?
- How are candy bars made? Could you make one at home? How would you go about making one?
- Can candy be made without sugar? How does it taste? If you were blindfolded and told to eat a candy bar, could you tell what type it was? How would you identify it?

---

**Focus Question...**
- What is the average price of a candy bar in the United States today? Do you think it would cost more or less in Japan? In France? In Russia? Why do you think so?
- How many candy bars would you need if everyone in this class was to receive one?

---

**Problem...**
Lizzie and Rita would like to buy a 35-cent candy bar for each student present in class today. What will their total cost be?

# HOW MUCH FOR CANDY BARS FOR EVERYONE?

## Objectives
- to represent and solve problems using geometric models
- to develop confidence in solving linear equations using concrete, informal, and formal methods
- to develop number sense for whole numbers, decimals, integers, and rational numbers

## Graphing
First, ask the students to list the cost of from 1 to 11 candy bars. Order is important for visualizing patterns.

| # Bars | 1 | 2 | 3 | 4 | 5 | 6 | 7 | 8 | 9 | 10 | 11 |
|--------|-----|-----|------|------|------|------|------|------|------|------|------|
| $ Cost | .35 | .70 | 1.05 | 1.40 | 1.75 | 2.10 | 2.45 | 2.80 | 3.15 | 3.50 | 3.85 |

## Discussing
Ask the students if they can find several ways of showing or projecting the total cost for the entire class using information from the above table. (For purposes of demonstration, we will assume there are 28 students in the class.) One method might be to locate the known prices on a two-dimensional graph and project the class cost by extending the line, as shown below.

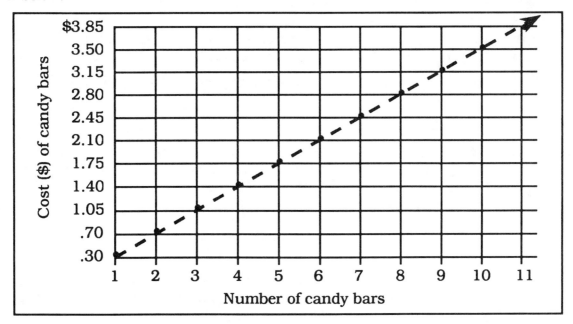

## Mathing
One way to find the total cost may be to quadruple the cost of 7 candy bars: 4 × 2.45 = $9.80. Another method would be to divide the group of 28 students into smaller units, such as 10 + 10 + 8, and project a total cost: $3.50 + 3.50 + 2.80 = $9.80.

## Answering
Multiply the number of students by $.35 for the total cost of the candy bars.

## Extending
If Lizzie and Rita live in a county where all sales are taxed 7%, how much will it cost them, including sales tax, to buy a candy bar for each student in the class?

---

# "SAVE $20 OFF THE COVER PRICE!"

### Initial Graph...
Choose your favorite news and wildlife magazines. Mark your choice on the chart below.

|          | Ranger Rick | Zoo Books | National Wildlife | Audubon |
|----------|-------------|-----------|-------------------|---------|
| Time     |             |           |                   |         |
| Newsweek |             |           |                   |         |

### Speaking of Magazines...
- What wildlife or news magazines are popular besides those listed above? What other special-interest areas can you think of that have their own magazines? Are any wildlife or news magazines published just for students? If so, name some.
- Are any of these magazines sold in other countries? Are they translated into different languages?
- Why would anyone buy news magazines? Don't they cover the same news that you hear on television or read in the newspaper?
- What major issues might be written about in wildlife magazines? Make up some headlines for stories that you think might be covered.

### Focus Question...
- What is the average cover price of the magazines above? How can you find out? How much would it cost you at a newsstand to buy one copy of each magazine you chose on the **Initial Graph**?

### Problem...
Every month Michelle buys a magazine called *Animals Forever*. It costs $1.75 per issue at the newsstand. In the last issue she bought, she saw the following advertisement. Is it correct? Can Michelle save $20 off the cover price?

---

**SAVE UP TO $20 OFF THE COVER PRICE**
**OF**
*ANIMALS FOREVER*

___ 6 month subscription for $9
___ 12 month subscription for $13
___ 18 month subscription for $18
___ 24 month subscription for $22

---

# "SAVE $20 OFF THE COVER PRICE!"

## Objectives
- to acquire confidence in using mathematics meaningfully
- to apply mathematical thinking and modeling to problems that arise in other areas
- to extend the understanding of whole-number operations to decimals

## Graphing
Several different graphs can be used to show the comparison costs. Encourage students to determine for themselves how to graphically justify their results.

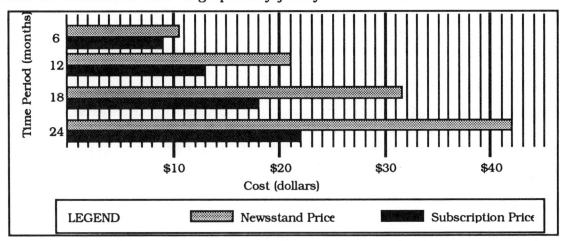

## Mathing
One approach may be to find the full newsstand cost for each time period mentioned.

| | |
|---|---|
| for 6 months:    6 × 1.75 = $10.50 | for 18 months:    18 × 1.75 = $31.50 |
| for 12 months:  12 × 1.75 = $21.00 | for 24 months:    24 × 1.75 = $42.00 |

Then subtract the special subscription cost and compare the savings with $20.00.

| | | |
|---|---|---|
| for 6 months: | 10.50 – 9.00 = | $ 1.50 savings |
| for 12 months: | 21.00 – 13.00 = | 8.00 savings |
| for 18 months: | 31.50 – 18.00 = | 13.50 savings |
| for 24 months: | 42.00 – 22.00 = | 20.00 savings |

Another way of approaching this problem is to calculate the subscription price per magazine by dividing the subscription rate by the time period.

| | | |
|---|---|---|
| $9.00 ÷ 6 = $1.50 month | .25 savings/month for 6 months | 6 × .25 = $1.50 savings |
| $13.00 ÷ 12 = $1.08 month | .67 savings/month for 12 months | 12 × .67 = $8.04 savings |
| $18.00 ÷ 18 = $1.00 month | .75 savings/month for 18 months | 18 × .75 = $13.50 savings |
| $22.00 ÷ 24 = $.92 month | .83 savings/month for 24 months | 24 × .83 = $19.92 savings |

## Discussing
Encourage students to speculate on reasons for the price differentials. What method did students use to justify the amount of savings? The amounts differ because the rounding of small amounts were magnified several times. For example, had the decimal been carried out two more places on the 24-month subscription price, the per-issue cost would have been .9167, which is .8333 savings per month, and 24 × .8333 = $19.9992. But since subscriptions are paid as a lump sum rather than monthly, $20 is the true savings.

## Answering
Yes, with a two-year subscription it is possible to save $20 off the cover price.

## Extending
Develop special subscription rates for a magazine that sells for $2.50 at the newsstand.

# PICTURE FRAMES

## Initial Graph...
Mark your response on the graph below.

### For Our Class Picture, I Would Like To:

| Leave it unframed | Frame it with glass | Frame it without glass |
| --- | --- | --- |
| | | |

## Speaking of Picture Frames...
- How much would an inexpensive 8" x 10" frame cost? Where could you buy one? Where could you go in this area for quality frames? Where might you look to find a store that specializes in picture frames?
- What choices might you have to make when framing a picture? Color? Size? Type of glass, if any? Style of frame? What else?
- How many framed pictures are in your home? How large do you think the biggest one is? What do you think the smallest one measures?
- If you worked as a picture framer, how could you get people interested in your product?

## Focus Question...
- If the class picture was square in shape and you wanted to frame it, would you have to use a square frame? How much larger than the picture would you like a frame to be?

## Problem...
Alida wants to frame a picture. The picture is a 5 x 5 square, and the frame is 1 unit wide. What fractional part of the complete 7 x 7 square is the frame?

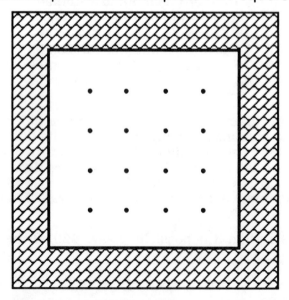

# PICTURE FRAMES

### Objectives
- to generalize solutions and strategies to new problem situations
- to investigate relationships among fractions, decimals, and percents
- to understand, represent, and use numbers in a variety of equivalent forms in real-world and mathematical problem situations
- to develop number sense for whole numbers and fractions

### Materials
Interlocking cubes or grid paper for students who have difficulty visualizing the problem

### Graphing
The problem is easily extended into a sequence of fractions for frames of various sized squares. Begin with the smallest possible square picture (1 x 1), frame it, and compare the number of squares in the frame to the entire number of squares.

$$\frac{\text{8 squares in the shaded frame}}{\text{9 squares in the entire diagram}}$$

Continue for the next four increased-size square picture. The fraction of the framework is indicated below each diagram.

     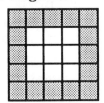     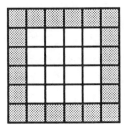     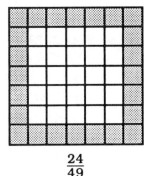

$$\frac{12}{16} \qquad\qquad \frac{16}{25} \qquad\qquad \frac{20}{36} \qquad\qquad \frac{24}{49}$$

### Mathing
How do the fractions change each time? The numerator increases by four. There are several ways to note the change in the denominator. Some students will notice square numbers ($3 \times 3$, $4 \times 4$, $5 \times 5$, $6 \times 6$, $7 \times 7$). Others will see the increase by addition,

$$9 + 7 = 16 \qquad 16 + 9 = 25 \qquad 25 + 11 = 36 \qquad 36 + 13 = 49$$

recognizing that consecutive odd numbers are added to previous denominators.

### Discussing
Encourage the students to explain their methods of attacking this problem and to discuss difficulties they encountered in visualizing the changes in the sizes of the picture and frame.

### Answering
The picture frame is $\frac{24}{49}$ of the entire square.

### Extending
- What fractional part would a one-unit frame be if it surrounded a picture 100 x 100?
- Would the fractional pattern change if the picture and frame were rectangular? For example, if the picture was 1 x 2 with a one-unit frame, what fractional part of the entire rectangle would the frame be then? Extend the size of the picture. Does a pattern develop?

---

# EGGSHELL THICKNESS

**Initial Graph...**
Mark your response to the question in the diagram below.

### I Like To:

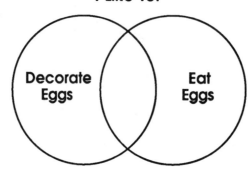

_____

**Speaking of Eggs...**
- How do you break the shell of an egg if you want to eat the egg? Does it make a difference whether the egg is raw or hard boiled? How does this differ from the way you would prepare an egg to decorate? How can you get the insides out of an egg without cracking the shell into pieces?
- What different types of eggs are there? Are they all edible? Can they all be decorated? Would it be harder to break an ostrich egg or a chicken egg? Why do you think so?
- Do eggs from different animals have shells of different size? Thickness? Strength? Color?
- What animals, if any, break the shells of eggs they eat? How do they do it? Do any animals eat eggs without breaking the shell? How do they do that?

_____

**Focus Question...**
- How might you determine the size of an egg? How might you measure the thickness of an eggshell?

_____

**Problem...**
Evan has been buying eggs from a nearby chicken farm. When he was making breakfast yesterday, he found that one of the eggs was hard to break. The shell appeared to be too thick to break easily! How thick do you think the average eggshell is?

# EGGSHELL THICKNESS

## Objectives
- to use computation, estimation, and proportions to solve problems
- to estimate, make, and use measurements to describe and compare phenomena
- to extend students' understanding of the process of measurement
- to select appropriate units and tools for measuring to the degree of accuracy required in a particular situation
- to understand the structure and use of systems of measurement

## Materials
For each group of students, you will need scratch paper, rulers, and an egg shell (broken, cleaned, and dried).

## Discussing
Place students in groups of three or four and give each group scratch paper, rulers, and egg shells. Tell each group they are to arrive at one measured estimate for the thickness of their shell using only the materials they have, although they may further break up the eggshells if they wish. It is important that students hear several different methods or ways of approaching the problem. Encourage them to discuss any difficulty they experienced when measuring, especially when measuring a stack of curved pieces.

After each group has agreed upon the thickness of its shell, write the groups' responses on the chalkboard. Ask members of each group to explain how they arrived at their responses.

## Mathing
Some groups might stack broken pieces up to the one-inch mark, count the number of pieces, and divide. Other groups might stack broken pieces to the one-quarter or one-eighth inch mark and go from there. Some might stack ten pieces of shell and measure that. Others might concentrate on one shell piece and estimate the thickness visually on the ruler. This last method is certainly not as accurate as the others.

## Graphing
Ask each group to mark the value closest to its estimates from the measurements on a line graph similar to the one below. Each answer should be close to $\frac{1}{100}$.

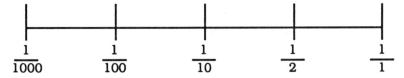

$$\frac{1}{1000} \qquad \frac{1}{100} \qquad \frac{1}{10} \qquad \frac{1}{2} \qquad \frac{1}{1}$$

## Answering
The average eggshell has a thickness of $\frac{1}{100}$ inch.

## Extending
- Is it possible for a group to have an answer with a numerator greater than one? How could that happen? What does it mean?
- How many inches would 1000 pieces of stacked eggshell measure? 2000?
- How thick is a blade of grass?

# GOLDEN RATIO

### Initial Graph...
Which of the following fractions best expresses the ratio of the length of your hand to the length of your arm?  Circle your choice below.

$$\frac{1}{2} \quad \frac{2}{2} \quad \frac{3}{2} \quad \frac{4}{2} \quad \frac{1}{3} \quad \frac{2}{3} \quad \frac{3}{3} \quad \frac{4}{3} \quad \frac{1}{4} \quad \frac{2}{4} \quad \frac{3}{4} \quad \frac{4}{4}$$

### Speaking of Ratios...
- What does the frational ratio you chose above express?  How can it be confirmed?  How does it compare with the fractional ratio of the length of your foot to the length of your leg?
- Can different fractions represent the same ratio?  If so, can you find two or more fractions above that represent the same ratio?
- How does one-fourth compare to the other ratios listed above?  What items do you see in this room that can be expressed in a ratio equal to one-fourth?

### Focus Question...
- Do you see a pattern in the way the fractions are listed in the **Initial Graph**?  Could you arrange those fractions in order from smallest to largest?  Do you see a different pattern in this new arrangement?  Now arrange the fractions in a different way.  How are they related this time?

### Problem...
Winona read about a famous sequence of numbers in math, called the "Fibonacci numbers," where the first two terms are one and each term after that is the sum of the two terms before it:

$$1, 1, 2, 3, 5, 8, 13, 21, 34, 55, 89, \cdots$$

In other words, $1 + 1 = 2$, $1 + 2 = 3$, $2 + 3 = 5$, $3 + 5 = 8$, $5 + 8 = 13$, and so on.

She used the Fibonacci sequence to form these fractions.

$$\frac{1}{1}, \ \frac{2}{1}, \ \frac{3}{2}, \ \frac{5}{3}, \ \frac{8}{5}, \ \frac{13}{8}, \ \frac{21}{13}, \ \frac{34}{21}, \ \frac{55}{34}, \ \frac{89}{55}$$

What would be the next fraction in her sequence?

$\dfrac{89}{144}$ _____  $\dfrac{55}{89}$ _____

$\dfrac{144}{89}$ _____  $\dfrac{89}{55}$ _____

none of the above _____

# GOLDEN RATIO

## Objectives
- to investigate relationships among fractions, decimals, and percents
- to analyze functional relationships to explain how a change in one quantity results in a change in another
- to describe, extend, analyze, and create a wide variety of patterns

## Graphing
Encourage students to show any patterns graphically. For example, the denominator pattern might be shown as follows.

$$\frac{1}{1} \searrow \frac{2}{1} \searrow \frac{3}{2} \searrow \frac{5}{3} \searrow \frac{8}{5} \searrow \frac{13}{8} \searrow \frac{21}{13} \searrow \frac{34}{21}$$

The numerator pattern could then be graphed in the manner shown to the right.

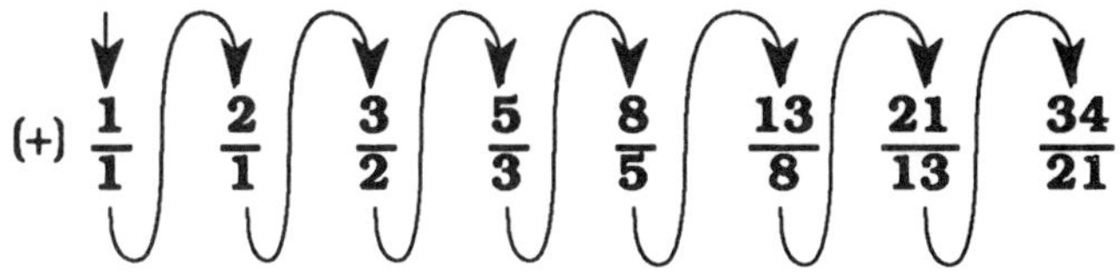

$$(+) \quad \frac{1}{1} \quad \frac{2}{1} \quad \frac{3}{2} \quad \frac{5}{3} \quad \frac{8}{5} \quad \frac{13}{8} \quad \frac{21}{13} \quad \frac{34}{21}$$

## Mathing
Since each number in the sequence is the sum of the two numbers immediately before it, the Fibonacci sequence can be extended as follows

1, 1, 2, 3, 5, 8, 13, 21, 34, 55, 89, 144 (55 + 89),...

The sequence of fractions is formed by the numerator being the next number in the Fibonacci sequence; the denominator is the number to the left of the numerator.

## Discussing
This problem should never stop with just one fraction. Observe what happens with the fractions (convergence) as the sequence extends.

## Answering
The next fraction in the sequence would be $\frac{144}{89}$.

## Extending
What happens if you change each fraction in the sequence to its decimal value? Is any pattern formed by this?

1

2

1.5

1.6666666...

1.6

1.625

1.6153846...

1.6190476...

1.6176471...

1.6181818...

1.6179775...

...

As the sequence of fractions continues, the number approachs a limit. That is, each gets closer and closer to a single, unique number. That number, in this instance, is known as the "Golden Ratio."

# PERIMETER TO AREA

**Initial Graph...**
Think of a rectangle that is 2 units by 1 unit. Mark the square on the graph below that indicates the dimensions of that rectangle.

**PERIMETER (units)**

| | 1 | 2 | 3 | 4 | 5 | 6 | 7 | 8 | 9 | 10 |
|---|---|---|---|---|---|---|---|---|---|---|
| 1 | | | | | | | | | | |
| 2 | | | | | | | | | | |
| 3 | | | | | | | | | | |
| 4 | | | | | | | | | | |
| 5 | | | | | | | | | | |
| 6 | | | | | | | | | | |
| 7 | | | | | | | | | | |
| 8 | | | | | | | | | | |
| 9 | | | | | | | | | | |
| 10 | | | | | | | | | | |

**AREA (square units)**

---

**Speaking of Dimensions...**
- What do we mean when we talk about the "area" of some object? What does "area" measure? When do we use area measurements?
- What do we mean when we talk about the "perimeter" of an object? What does "perimeter" measure? When might we use perimeter measurements in our daily lives?

---

**Focus Question...**
- A ratio can be made between the perimeter and the area of a rectangle. For instance, a rectangle with a perimeter of 4 units and an area of 1 unit has a ratio of 4 to 1 (perimeter to area). How would you express a ratio between the perimeter and area of a rectangle that is 2 units wide and 1 unit tall?

---

**Problem...**
Ché has drawn a 4 cm by 8 cm rectangle. What is the reduced fraction made by the ratio of his rectangle's perimeter to its area?

---

# PERIMETER TO AREA

## Objectives
- to extend students' understanding of the concepts of perimeter and area
- to understand the structure and use of systems of measurement
- to analyze functional relationships to explain how a change in one quantity results in a change in another

## Note
It may be necessary to review perimeter and area of rectangles before beginning the problem. Students may also find it helpful to sketch the rectangle's outline on a sheet of grid paper.

## Mathing
Ask students to explain how they found the measurements for Ché's rectangle. For perimeter, some may have drawn the rectangle and counted each unit around the outside. Others may have added the given length of the sides (4 + 8 + 4 + 8 = 24). The area could also be found by counting (32 squares) or by multiplication (4 × 8 = 32) or by addition (8 + 8 + 8 + 8 [or 4 + 4 + 4 + 4 + 4 + 4 + 4 + 4] = 32). The ratio of perimeter to area would then be 24 to 32, or $^{24}/_{32}$.

## Graphing
Ask students if they can show a pattern of perimeter-to-area relationships on a chart like the one started below. What happens if they reduce each ratio? Can they see any patterns?

Length of Rectangle

| | | ① | ② | ③ | ④ | ⑤ | ⑥ | ⑦ | ⑧ | ••• |
|---|---|---|---|---|---|---|---|---|---|---|
| | ① | $\frac{4}{1}$ | $\frac{6}{2}$ | $\frac{8}{3}$ | $\frac{10}{4}$ | $\frac{12}{5}$ | $\frac{14}{6}$ | $\frac{16}{7}$ | $\frac{18}{8}$ | |
| | ② | $\frac{6}{2}$ | $\frac{8}{4}$ | $\frac{10}{6}$ | $\frac{12}{8}$ | $\frac{14}{10}$ | $\frac{16}{12}$ | $\frac{18}{14}$ | $\frac{20}{16}$ | |
| Width of Rectangle | ③ | $\frac{8}{3}$ | $\frac{10}{6}$ | $\frac{12}{9}$ | $\frac{14}{12}$ | $\frac{16}{15}$ | $\frac{18}{18}$ | $\frac{20}{21}$ | $\frac{22}{24}$ | |
| | ④ | $\frac{10}{4}$ | $\frac{12}{8}$ | $\frac{14}{12}$ | $\frac{16}{16}$ | $\frac{18}{20}$ | $\frac{20}{24}$ | $\frac{22}{28}$ | $\frac{24}{32}$ | |
| | ⑤ | $\frac{12}{5}$ | $\frac{14}{10}$ | $\frac{16}{15}$ | $\frac{18}{20}$ | $\frac{20}{25}$ | $\frac{22}{30}$ | $\frac{24}{35}$ | $\frac{26}{40}$ | |
| | ⑥ | $\frac{14}{6}$ | $\frac{16}{12}$ | $\frac{18}{18}$ | $\frac{20}{24}$ | $\frac{22}{30}$ | $\frac{24}{36}$ | $\frac{26}{42}$ | $\frac{28}{48}$ | |
| | ⋮ | | | | | | | | | |

## Answering
The reduced ratio of the perimeter to area of a 4 cm by 8 cm rectangle is $^{3}/_{4}$.

## Extending
- Find a rectangular object in this room, measure its dimensions, and express its perimeter-to-area ratio as a reduced fraction.
- How does the ratio of a 2 unit by 1 unit rectangle change when the rectangle's length is doubled? Tripled?

# FRACTIONS ON A LINE

**Initial Graph...**
Make a mark to show where three and one-half is on the number line below.

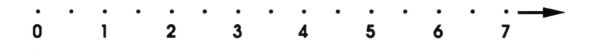

**Speaking of Number Lines...**
- What is a number line used for?  What can you tell about the numbers shown on that line?
- How is the three represented on the number line?  Where is it located in relation to the 2?  To the 7?
- What do the dots above the numbers represent?  What fraction do the dots between the numbers represent?
- What kinds of things are measured in terms of fractions?  Can you find examples of fractions in your math book?  In your English book?  In a newspaper?  In a magazine?

**Focus Question...**
- Can you find 3 ¼ on the number line above?  Where is it in relation to the three?  To the four?  How would you find three and three-fourths?

**Problem...**
Tian is trying to figure out where 3 and ⅝ would be located on the following number line. Can you help him? Place an **X** above the spot where you think the number would be.

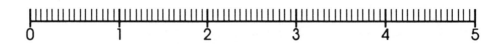

## FRACTIONS ON A LINE

### Objectives
- to extend students' understanding of the process of measurement
- to select appropriate units and tools for measuring to the degree of accuracy required in a particular situation
- to develop and use order relations for whole numbers, fractions, decimals, integers, and rational numbers

### Mathing
There are sixteen equal divisions between each whole number on the number line shown, similar to the number of divisions on a standard ruler. The problem as stated, however, is for 3 and ⅝ where the unit on the number line between 3 and 4 needs to be divided into 8 equal sections (indicated on the graph below by elongated lines). Five of those equal sections are counted from the direction of whole number 3 to 4, ending up at the fifth elongated line (or tenth line, if they were all short) to the right of the 3.

### Graphing
Encourage students to develop ways of showing "eights" on a line marked for "sixteenths."

### Discussion
What does "3 and ⅝" mean? What part is the "whole" and what part is the fraction? Look at each of the digits—the 3, the 5, and the 8—and explain how they are related.

### Answering
The spot for 3⅝ is indicated by the arrow above.

### Extending
- Draw a rectangle that is 3 ⅝ inches wide by 2 ³⁄₁₆ inches tall.
- How many fractions are there between whole numbers 3 and 4?

# VOWEL RATIOS

**Initial Graph...**
What vowels are in your first name? Mark the area in the diagram below that shows your response.

_____

**Speaking of Vowels...**
- How many vowels are in your first name? Can you think of a name with only one vowel? With two different vowels? With three? Four? Five? With all six?
- What spelling or grammar rules can you think of that involve vowels?
- Looking at a page in a dictionary, can you find any words that have no vowels? How many words can you find that have only one vowel? Which word(s) contain the greatest number of vowels? How many consonants are in that word?

_____

**Focus Question...**
- What patterns do you notice in the relationships between vowels and consonants in the words from the dictionary?

_____

**Problem...**
When Daisy wrote her name the other day, she noticed that her first name has 3 vowels (A, I, Y) and 5 total letters (D, A, I, S, Y). She put her name and the 3 and 5 in the columns below. Help her finish the chart. Write the name, the number of vowels, and the total number of letters in the first name of each student in your group.

| Name | Vowels | : | Letters |
|------|--------|---|---------|
| D A I S Y | 3 | : | 5 |
| | | : | |
| | | : | |
| | | : | |
| | | : | |
| | | : | |

# VOWEL RATIOS

## Objectives
- to systematically collect, organize, and describe data
- to construct, read, and interpret tables, charts, and graphs
- to make inferences and convincing arguments that are based on data analysis
- to develop an appreciation for statistical methods as a powerful decision-making tool

## Graphing
If students draw a line on the chalkboard and divide it into five equal parts, the ratio 3 : 5 can be shown at the end of the third part, with the name representing the whole of 5 parts. The letters in the name "Daisy" can then be rearranged to illustrate the ratio, as shown below.

3/5         5/5 or 1

Ask a student to demonstrate this approach with his or her name. A bar graph can also be used to represent any name. Place unit increments for vowels on the vertical axis and those for total number of letters on the horizontal axis.

## Mathing
The resulting ratio will always be the particular items selected divided by the total number of items involved. As shown, the number of vowels in a word is never more than the total number of letters in the word, although it is possible for them to be equal; for example, consider the following words: *eye, I, aye, a,* and *you*

## Discussing
What did the class notice about the examples of ratio given in the form of segments? (For example, in the case of DAISY the ratio is represented as a heavy bar just past the halfway point. In the case of DAN, it is just under halfway. In the case of PATRICIA, it is at the halfway point.) Do any of the other vowel : letter ratios form equal segments?

## Answering
A ratio is formed by each student counting the number of vowels and the total number of letters in his or her own name. Have each student also divide a line segment to demonstrate the concept of the ratio.

## Extending
- Are there any words which form a ratio of vowels to letters equal to one-half? Make a list of all such words found by the class.
- What about other words? In the word SATISFIED, the ratio bar is just before the halfway point. It appears that the ratio of vowels to total letters in words approaches one-half. Open a book to a random page and select ten words. Count the **total** letters in the ten words, then count the **total** number of vowels. What is the ratio of vowels to letters using the words? Combine the results into a ratio representing all the words counted by the entire class. Other letters in words are consonants. What would their ratio be to the total?

# PAINTING A ROOM TOGETHER

**Initial Graph...**
How many hours do you think it would take you to paint this room? Mark your response on the chart below.

| # of hours | |
|---|---|
| 1 | |
| 2 | |
| 3 | |
| 4 | |
| 5 | |
| 6 | |
| 7 | |
| 8 | |
| 9 | |
| 10 | |
| >10 | |

**Speaking of Painting a Room...**
- What would you have to do to get ready to paint this room tomorrow? What color would you paint the walls? Would you paint the ceiling? Would it be the same color as the walls? Why or why not? What parts of the room would not need to be painted?
- What types of paint are available for painting walls? What are the advantages and disadvantages of each? What other tools, supplies, or equipment would you need?
- How many gallons of paint do you think you would need to paint this room? Where could you buy the paint? How much would it cost for each gallon? For the whole room?
- What kinds of things would you have to do when you had finished painting the room? How long would it take you to do these things?

**Focus Question...**
- If someone in your class painted at about the same rate as you, how long do you think it would take to paint the room if you worked together?

**Problem...**
Martha says she can paint an average room in four hours by herself. Finnley, who just doesn't like to paint, says he could paint the same room in twelve hours by himself—if he wanted to. How long would it take them to paint the room if they worked together and each painted at the speed they claimed?

# PAINTING A ROOM TOGETHER

## Objectives
- to acquire confidence in using mathematics meaningfully
- to appreciate the value of mathematical notation and its role in the development of mathematical ideas
- to validate personal thinking
- to apply mathematical thinking and modeling to problems that arise in other disciplines
- to understand and apply ratios, proportions, and percents in a wide variety of situations
- to understand, represent, and use numbers in a variety of equivalent forms in real-world and mathematical problem situations

## Graphing
One method for solving the problem is to consider the room to be square, with each wall taking the same amount of time to paint. Since Martha is a fast worker, she would be done with ¼ of the room (one complete wall) in one hour. Finnley would do 1/12 of the room (4/12 or ⅓ of a wall) each hour. By making an hourly diagram, students can show that the room would be completely painted at the end of the third hour.

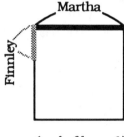
(end of hour 1)

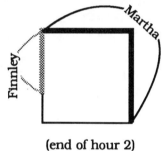
(end of hour 2)

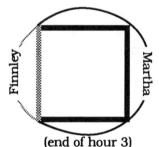
(end of hour 3)

## Mathing
Another approach is to consider the ratio of the amount of the job completed by Martha and Finnley separately. If it takes $n$ hours to complete the job, then the part of all the walls that Martha painted is $n/4$ and the part of the walls that Finnley painted is $n/12$. Together, they complete one job.

$$\frac{n}{4} + \frac{n}{12} = \frac{3 \times n}{3 \times 4} + \frac{n}{12} = \frac{4n}{12} = 1 \text{ job}$$

The above equation can be solved for $n = 3$.

## Discussing
Ask students to justify any given solution by showing either segments or shaded portions and comparing their counts. May the walls be joined or flattened as a huge rectangle?

## Answering
It would take 3 hours for Martha and Finnley to paint the room if they worked together.

## Extending
What if a third person, who could paint the room in 10 hours, would like to help? If all three worked together, how many hours and minutes would it take for the three of them to completely paint the room?

---

# NATURAL JUICE IN FRUIT PUNCH

**Initial Graph...**
Which of the following would you prefer to drink? Mark your choice on the graph below.

| | Soda |
|---|---|
| | Milk |
| | Juice |
| | Tea |
| | Coffee |
| | Water |
| | Hot Chocolate |

**Speaking of Beverages...**
- What things determine what beverage we drink? Does cost have an effect? Taste? Weather conditions? Holiday customs? Advertising?
- Which beverage on the **Initial Graph** do you think is the most expensive? Which is the least expensive? Which has the fewest calories? The most calories? Which is the most popular with you and your classmates? The least popular?
- What flavors are available in juice, tea, or soda? Sometimes soda and juice are mixed. What flavors are generally put together? Describe a new flavor you might make by mixing soda and juice or two kinds of juices.

**Focus Question...**
- Look at the label on a beverage container. What information does it give you? Does it tell you how many individual servings are in the container? What vitamins and minerals are in the beverage? What are the ingredients of the beverage (what is it made of)?

**Problem...**
Fiver has recently been drinking a new fruit punch. The label says that there are three (3) ounces of natural juice in a 15-ounce can. The rest of the punch is made up of carbonated water, citric acid, potassium benzoate, and potassium sorbate.

If Fiver drinks 5 ounces of this fruit punch for lunch, how many ounces of natural juice will he drink?

# NATURAL JUICE IN FRUIT PUNCH

## Objectives
- to acquire confidence in using mathematics meaningfully
- to appreciate the value of mathematical notation and its role in the development of mathematical ideas
- to validate personal thinking
- to apply mathematical thinking and modeling to problems that arise in other disciplines
- to understand and apply ratios, proportions, and percents in a wide variety of situations
- to understand, represent, and use numbers in a variety of equivalent forms (integer, fraction, decimal, percent, exponential, and scientific notation) in real-world and mathematical problem situations

## Graphing
Even though the contents are measured in volume, a diagram representing the side view of a can of fruit punch can be used to show amounts. The following diagram shows that there would be one ounce of natural juice in each five ounces of the fruit punch.

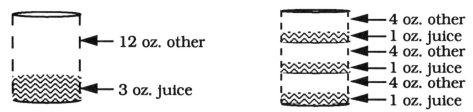

## Mathing
A solution by means of ratio uses the ratio of natural juice to fruit punch ( $3/15$ ), which is also the ratio for the amount of natural juice to other ingredients in each ounce of fruit punch. Since Fiver drank five ounces:

$$\frac{3}{15} + \frac{3}{15} + \frac{3}{15} + \frac{3}{15} + \frac{3}{15} = \frac{15}{15} = 1 \text{ ounce natural juice in 5 ounces of the punch.}$$

The problem can also be thought of as $3/15$ of 5 ounces, or $3/15 \times 5 = 1$.

## Discussing
Ask the students to explain how they determined the exact number of ounces of natural juice in the punch. Listen carefully to the methods each student or group used to solve the problem and encourage the class to question and comment on the techniques.

## Answering
If Fiver drinks 5 ounces of the new fruit punch, he will drink 1 ounce of natural juice.

## Extending
Suppose you made a party snack by mixing 1 cup of pretzels, 2 cups of cut celery, 1 cup of walnuts, and 3 cups of toasted wheat cereal. Your guests didn't seem to like this mixture very well and left 5 cups untouched. How many cups of celery would you have left?

# COMPARING FOOTSTEPS

**Initial Graph...**
If you walked across the room (from the door to the opposite side) in a normal way, how many footsteps do you think it would take you? Write your estimate on the line below.

_____

**Speaking of Walking...**
- What is the average distance between footsteps (from the toe of the back foot to the heel of the front foot) in the class? How can we find out? What is that distance in metric measurements? Does the distance change when you are in a hurry?
- Is there a relationship between the length of your footsteps and the length of your legs?
- Do athletes walk with longer strides? What sort of exercises might make your strides longer?
- When you walk, do you come down on your toes or your heels? Does that change when you run? If so, how? How and why are running shoes built differently from walking shoes?

_____

**Focus Question...**
- What would you think the average distance between footsteps might be for a three-year-old child? How does that compare to your footsteps? If you took ten steps, how many steps would that three year old take to cover the same distance?

_____

**Problem...**
Dottie went for a walk with her uncle yesterday. She found that she took 3 steps for every 2 that her uncle took. If Dottie's uncle walked 100 steps, how many steps did Dottie take walking beside him?

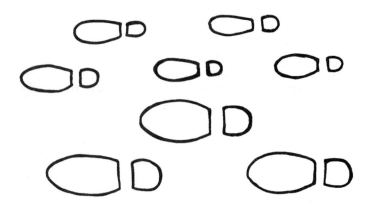

# COMPARING FOOTSTEPS

## Objectives
- to analyze functional relationships to explain how a change in one quantity results in a change in another
- to understand the structure and use of systems of measurement
- to systematically collect, organize, and describe data
- to describe and represent relationships with tables, graphs, and rules

## Graphing
This problem develops a ratio then takes it from a small case to a larger one. Ask two students to demonstrate what is taking place, with one student playing the part of Dottie and another her uncle. Let the "uncle" take two steps, then "Dottie" will take three. If the "uncle" takes two more steps, "Dottie" will bring her total up to 6. Ask a student to record on the chalkboard what is happening.

| Total steps by uncle | 2 | 4 | 6 | 8 | 10 | 12 | 14 | 16 | 18 | 20 | 22 | 24 | 26 | 28 | ... |
|---|---|---|---|---|---|---|---|---|---|---|---|---|---|---|---|
| Total steps by Dottie | 3 | 6 | 9 | 12 | 15 | 18 | 21 | 24 | 27 | 30 | 33 | 36 | 39 | 42 | ... |

Another approach to graphing this problem is to divide a line segment to show "steps."

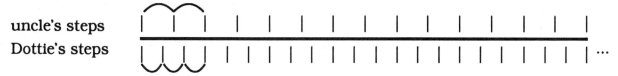

## Mathing
Using the numeric graph, students may see a pattern forming; i.e., the top line is the multiples of 2 and the bottom line is the multiples of 3. We could have stopped at 20 of the uncle's steps, which is one-fifth of the desired distance (100), then multiplied Dottie's steps (30) by 5 to find the total (150 steps).

Students who use the line-segment graph may also see a pattern forming:

2 uncle's steps means 3 Dottie's steps; so...

20 (2 × 10) uncle's steps means 30 (3 × 10) Dottie's steps;

40 (20 × 2) uncle's steps means 60 (30 × 2) Dottie's steps;

80 (40 × 2) uncle's steps means 120 (60 × 2) Dottie's steps;

100 (80 + 20) uncle's steps means 150 (120 + 30) Dottie's steps.

Retrospect shows that it would have been possible to go from the first step to the last step by multiplying by 50.

Encourage students to try to form an equation they could apply to any number of steps taken by the uncle and find the number of steps taken by Dottie. For example,

if $s$ = number of uncle's steps, then ($s/2$) × 3 = number of Dottie's steps.

## Discussing
On what multiples of 2 and 3 would both Dottie and her uncle step together? During the intervals between each of these "together" steps, how many steps would Dottie take? How many would her uncle take?

## Answering
If her uncle walks 100 steps, Dottie will take 150 steps walking beside him.

## Extending
If Dottie had taken 30 steps more than her uncle as they walked side by side, how many steps would her uncle have taken?

# HEIGHT OF A TREE

## Initial Graph...

If a stick stuck straight up out of the ground, it would cast a shadow:

| Less than the stick's length | Equal to the stick's length | Greater than the stick's length |
|---|---|---|
| | | |

Mark your response on the chart above.

---

## Speaking of Shadows...

- What makes shadows change? What things determine the length of a shadow cast by a stick? Does the time of the day or season of the year make any difference?
- How do shadows change on a flat plain, a rolling hill, or a mountain side?
- What famous paintings have used shadows? Do you see any shadows in this room? Why or why not? Do you see any shadows outside? Why or why not?

---

## Focus Question...

- How do shadows of sticks, people, trees, and buildings compare with each other? Does the longest shadow always indicate the tallest object?

---

## Problem...

MacKenzie, who was riding her horse in a flat field, noted a stick standing 25 inches straight out of the ground. It cast a 35-inch shadow behind it. A nearby tree, also standing straight up toward the sky, cast a shadow of 105 feet. How tall was the tree? Mark an **X** on the line beside the vertical distance which you think comes closest to showing the height of the tree.

- — 200 feet
- — 180 feet
- — 160 feet
- — 140 feet
- — 120 feet
- — 100 feet
- — 80 feet
- — 60 feet
- — 40 feet
- — 20 feet
- — 0 feet

# HEIGHT OF A TREE

## Objectives
- to estimate, make, and use measurements to describe and compare phenomena
- to develop, analyze, and explain methods for solving proportions
- to understand and apply ratios and proportions in a wide variety of situations
- to understand, represent, and use numbers in a variety of equivalent forms in real-world and mathematical problem situations

## Graphing
It may help students to draw a picture of the problem. A diagram like the one shown here allows for two similar triangles and helps line up similar sides.

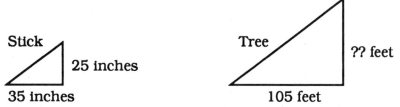

## Mathing
If $h$ represents the height of the tree, ask students how they might proceed. With the numbers lined up, as shown above, they may set up ratios:

$$\frac{25 \text{ in.}}{35 \text{ in.}} = \frac{h \text{ ft.}}{105 \text{ ft.}} \qquad \frac{25 \times 3}{35 \times 3} = \frac{75}{105} = \frac{h}{105}, \text{ thus } h = 75 \text{ feet.}$$

If students have calculators, this ratio equation could be solved by first dividing (25 ÷ 35 = .7142857) then multiplying (.7142857 × 105 = 74.99999); or by first multiplying (25 × 105 = 2625) then dividing (2625 ÷ 35 = 75).

## Discussing
This problem illustrates using two ratios with one unknown. Ask students to justify their solution by explaining how they arrived at their answer. They might have enlarged the first stick-and-shadow diagram (above) three times, justifying inches/inches = feet/feet, as shown here.

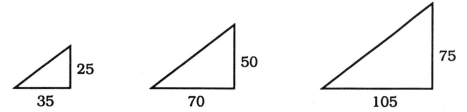

## Answering
The height of the tree was 75 feet, so the closest mark on the line would have been 80.

## Extending
Put a stick in your hand and make it the same length as the distance from your eye to your hand. Extend your arm straight out and, holding the end of the stick in your hand, point it straight up. Then, looking at a tree, back up until you can just barely see the top branch over the end of the stick. Now, by measuring how far you are standing from the foot of the tree, determine how tall the tree is. (The tree height will be approximately the same as your distance from the tree; this is a frequently-used outdoor method for determining heights of trees.)

# APPLES, RED OR GREEN?

**Initial Graph...**
How many different varieties of apples can you name? Write your list below
(and don't worry about the spelling).

_____    _____

_____    _____

_____    _____

_____    _____

_____    _____

_____

**Speaking of Apples...**
- Apples have been known around the world for a long time, as shown by
  their mention in early myths, legends, and poems. Can you think of any
  fairy tales or myths that involved apples? What interesting historical
  information can you find about the apple? Where would you look to find
  this information?
- How many different uses can you think of for apples? Do all of those uses
  involve food? What else might you use an apple for? (Be creative.)
- Where do most of the apples sold in this area come from? Do they always
  come from the same place? Which states in the United States grow the
  most apples? What country in Europe grows the most apples?

_____

**Focus Question...**
- How are apples grown? What kinds of diseases or bugs attack apple trees
  and their fruit? Are any other fruits related to the apple?

_____

**Problem...**
The produce store in Sweethome has both red apples and green apples.
Russell says the green apples taste better because they are tart and firm. Bill
argues that the red ones taste better because they are sweet and juicy.

Do you agree with Russell and prefer tart, firm, green apples or with Bill and
prefer sweet, juicy, red apples? Place an **X** under the column of your choice.

| Tart, green apples | Sweet, red apples |
|---|---|
|  |  |

# APPLES, RED OR GREEN?

## Objectives

- to systematically collect, organize, and describe data
- to develop an appreciation for statistical methods as a powerful decision-making tool
- to develop and apply number-theory concepts (e.g., primes, factors, multiples) in real-world and mathematical problem situations
- to understand and appreciate the need for numbers beyond the whole numbers

## Graphing

Record the statistics on a class graph, then ask the students what they might do with the information they've gathered. Let's assume that our sample records the following choices.

| Tart, green apples | Sweet, red apples |
|:---:|:---:|
| 9 | 19 |

## Mathing

One use of the above information is to add 9 + 19, showing that there are a total of 28 recorded choices. Subtraction (19 – 9) shows that there are 10 more students who prefer red apples. These can be shown immediately by cutting out 9 green and 19 red apples from construction paper and lining them up on a chalkboard to show the sum or by placing the red paper apples in a line directly below the green ones, demonstrating the difference as those apples that are beyond corresponding pairs of green and red.

The above information can also be used to show ratio relationships:

- $9/19$ is the green to red preference for apples;
- $19/9$ is the red to green preference for apples;
- $9/28$ is the tart, green apple preference for the total class;
- $19/28$ is the sweet, red apple preference for the total class.

These last two ratios divide the entire class (28) into two parts:

$$\frac{9}{28} + \frac{19}{28} = \frac{28}{28} = 1 \text{ class}$$

Ratios can also be changed to decimal form (.32 + .68 = 1), where multiplication by 100 results in 32 + 68 = 100, and 32 represents the part of 100 people who prefer green apples and 68 represents the part of 100 people who prefer red apples.

Percentage, a mathematical term for "the part out of 100," can demonstrate that:

- 32% of the class prefers tart, green apples to sweet, red apples.
- 68% of the class prefers sweet, red apples to tart, green apples.

## Discussing

This problem introduces percent by dividing a sample into two parts. (Making the choice between type of apples is not the purpose of the problem, and you needn't dwell on color or taste.) Ask students, if they had equal numbers of red and green apples, what percentage would be green? Would it make any difference how many apples they had? If they had twice as many green apples as red ones, what percentage would be green? Red? Again, does the total number of apples make any difference?

## Answering

Use the information recorded in this problem to demonstrate percent.

## Extending

Make a chart like the following on the chalkboard. Ask each person, in turn, to put an **X** under his or her hair color. What can students do with this information?

| Red hair | Black hair | Brown hair | Blonde hair |
|:---:|:---:|:---:|:---:|

## SALAD AND DESSERT EATERS

### Initial Graph...
How do you prefer to eat most vegetables?  Mark your response in the area of the graph that shows your choice.

**I prefer to eat most vegetables:**

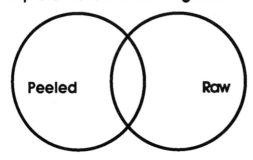

### Speaking of Vegetables...
- If everyone in the class made his or her mark on the same graph, how many total responses would we have on that graph?
- If there were one mark in each section of the diagram above (see below), what percentage of the total would like raw vegetables? Peeled vegetables?  Both raw and peeled vegetables?  Neither?

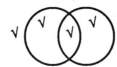

### Focus Question...
- Let's mark the class choices on a diagram on the chalkboard.  Can we use this information to find out what percentage of this class prefers raw vegetables?  Peeled vegetables?  Both raw and peeled?
- Do any people in this class like neither raw nor peeled vegetables?  How is that percentage related to those we found in the last question?

### Problem...
Yoko was at a picnic last weekend with 100 guests.  Of the guests at the picnic,
        64 ate salad,
        41 ate salad and dessert, and
        52 ate dessert.

What percent of the guests ate neither salad nor dessert?  See if you can graph your answer.

# SALAD AND DESSERT EATERS

## Objectives
- to appreciate the use and power of reasoning as a part of mathematics
- to investigate relationships among fractions, decimals, and percents
- to represent situations and number patterns with tables, graphs, verbal rules, and equations and to explore the interrelationships of these representations
- to use computation, estimation, and proportions to solve problems

## Graphing
One approach might be to consider a 100-unit strip of paper to be the 100 guests. Tear (or mark) off 41 units to represent the guests who ate both salad and dessert. Since a total of 64 ate salad, 23 more are needed to represent total salad eaters. Since a total of 52 ate dessert, 11 more (than the 41) are needed to represent dessert eaters. This will leave 25 units on the strip of paper, representing those who ate neither salad nor dessert.

Another approach may be to use a Venn diagram similar to the one used in the initial graph.

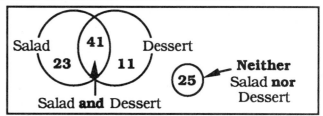

## Mathing
One approach might be to divide the 64 into two sets:

      41 ate salad and dessert

      64 – 41 = 23 ate salad, but no dessert

and then divide the 52 into two sets:

      41 ate salad and dessert

      52 – 41 = 11 ate dessert, but no salad

Thus, the three subsets of guests mentioned above ate either salad or dessert or both. So,

        41   (salad and dessert)

        23   (salad, but no dessert)

    + 11   (dessert, but no salad)

        75   TOTAL guests ate dessert and/or salad

leaving 25 of the 100 guests (25%) who ate neither.

## Discussing
The purpose of this problem is to divide a group into intersecting subsets and find the remainder in percent. Ask students to explain how they proceeded in solving this problem. Did they notice that of the 64 guests who ate salad, 41 also ate dessert? Did they notice that of the 52 guests who ate dessert, 41 also ate salad?

## Answering
Of the guests, 25% ate neither salad nor dessert.

## Extending
How many guests were at a party if, of all the guests, 13 ate cookies, 7 ate cookies and candy, 10 ate candy, and 20% of the guests ate neither candy nor cookies?

## DISTANCE TO KANSAS

**Initial Graph...**
How far do you think it is from our school to the state capital? Mark your estimate on the graph below.

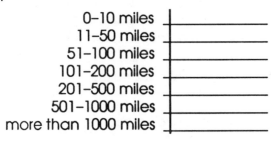

0–10 miles
11–50 miles
51–100 miles
101–200 miles
201–500 miles
501–1000 miles
more than 1000 miles

**Speaking of Mileage...**
- What source could you go to to find out the exact mileage from here to the state capital?
- Look at a state road map. How is mileage shown on this map? What is the scale on the map?
- How far is it from school to the closest large city? How does that distance compare to the distance to the capital city?

**Focus Question...**
- What is the shortest route from here to the state capital? How long would it take to drive it?

**Problem...**
A local map shows the distance from Liu's cabin to Sweethome as this far:

Cabin        Sweethome

Liu knows that the distance from his cabin to Sweethome is 30% of the distance from his cabin to the next largest city, Kansas. How far on that same map would it be from his cabin to Kansas? Put an **X** in the box beside the line (A, B, C, or D) that would show the distance from the cabin to Kansas.

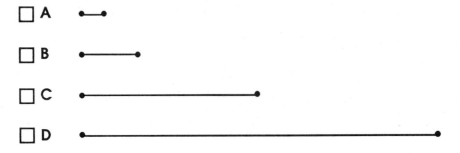

☐ A

☐ B

☐ C

☐ D

## DISTANCE TO KANSAS

### Objectives
- to develop number sense for whole numbers, fractions, decimals, integers, and rational numbers
- to represent numerical relationships on one-dimensional graphs

### Graphing
Ask students how they could find the larger distance exactly. One method is to triple the given length from the cabin to Sweethome (3 × 30% = 90%), then add one-third of the given length:

$$(3 \times 30\% + (\tfrac{1}{3})\,30\% = 90\% + 10\% = 100\%).$$

●———————●··········●———————●··●

### Mathing
Another approach is to break the 30% into three 10% "pieces" (10 is a factor of 100 and 30 is not a factor of 100). 10 × 10% = 100%.

### Discussing
The purpose of this problem is to relate percentage to a linear distance. Ask the students to clarify the problem. *"What distance is Liu looking for? What relationships do you know from the problem statement?"* The unknown distance is **not** 30% of the distance from the cabin to Sweethome, but rather **that distance itself** is 30% of a greater distance.

### Answering
The distance from Liu's cabin to Kansas is represented by segment **C**.

### Extending
- The distance from Liu's cabin to Sweethome is 140% of what length?
- Relate this knowledge of percentage and distance to numbers. For example, consider the problem:

    **$6 is 30% of what amount?**

The $6 now replaces a linear distance from the cabin to Sweethome in the original problem. If that distance represents $6,

    $ $ $ $ $ $     (distance of the cabin to Sweethome),

then the final result is the length represented from the cabin to Kansas.

    $ $ $ $ $ $|$ $ $ $ $ $|$ $ $ $ $ $|$ $        (distance from the cabin to Kansas)

Each small sign represents $1, so the total is twenty dollars. $6 is 30% of $20.

# HOME PETS

### Initial Graph...
Do you have any pets living in your home?  Mark the diagram below to show the area that represents your answer.

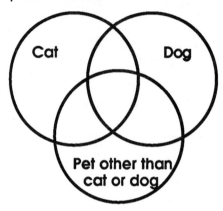

---

### Speaking of Pets...
- Why do some families choose not to have pets in their home?
- What types of pets might people have besides cats or dogs?  Are there restrictions on the types of pets you can have where you live?  If so, who determines those restrictions?
- How much does it cost per year to keep a dog or a cat?  What type of expenses might these include?

---

### Focus Question...
- What part of the class has pets?  What part of the class does not have a pet in their home?
- What percentage of the class has a cat?  A dog?  Both?  A pet other than a cat or dog?  What percentage of the class has a cat, a dog, and another type of pet?  What percentage of the class has no pet in their home?

---

### Problem...
Nydia, who attends a school that has 75 students, read that 4% of the population does not have a pet at home.  If the students in her school followed this national average, how many of those 75 **do** have a pet in their home?  Can you graph your results?

# HOME PETS

## Objectives

- to explore problems and describe results using graphical, numerical, physical, algebraic, and verbal mathematical models or representations
- to understand and apply ratios, proportions, and percents in a wide variety of situations
- to develop number sense for whole numbers, fractions, decimals, integers, and rational numbers
- to understand, represent, and use numbers in a variety of equivalent forms in real-world and mathematical problem situations
- to develop and use order relations for whole numbers, fractions, decimals, integers, and rational numbers

## Graphing

One method is to break down the 4% of nonpet owners. 4% means "4 out of 100" which, as a ratio, can be reduced to 1 out of every 25 people who are not pet owners. If the sample of 75 students is divided into three equal groups of 25, one student in each group would not own a pet. Since there are three groups of 25, three of the 75 in the total sample would not, according to the national average, own a pet. It is easy to demonstrate this process using graph paper on the overhead.

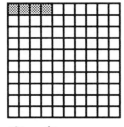

4% = ⁴/₁₀₀
nonpet owners

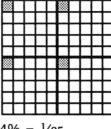

4% = ¹/₂₅
nonpet owners

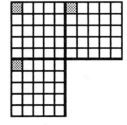

4% of 75 = 3
nonpet owners

Another approach to solving this problem might be to identify the national percentage of pet owners (100% – 4% = 96% pet owners), then proceed on a basis similar to the method above.

## Mathing

Demonstrate the numerical approach last:

> 4% of 75 = .04 × 75 = 3 nonpet owners
>
> 75 – 3 = 72 pet owners

>     **OR**
>
> 100% – 4% = 96% pet owners
>
> 96% of 75 = .96 × 75 = 72 pet owners

## Answering

According to the national average, 72 of the 75 students have a pet.

## Extending

The town of Sweethome has a population of 2456, and the average household has 2.8 people. Using the statistics from the original problem, how many **homes** should have at least one pet? (**Answer:** 96% of 2456 = .96 x 2456 = 2357.8 pet owners; 2357.8 ÷ 2.8 = 842 homes.) Make a graph that shows this information.

# CUTTING AWAY A TRIANGLE

## Initial Graph...

How many triangles do you see in the shape below? Mark your response beside the matching number on the graph below.

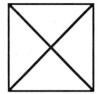

| | |
|---|---|
| 0 _____ | 5 _____ |
| 1 _____ | 6 _____ |
| 2 _____ | 7 _____ |
| 3 _____ | 8 _____ |
| 4 _____ | 9 _____ |

## Speaking of Triangles...

- How many different kinds of triangles are there? What determines the name of a triangle, the sides or the angles?

- What is the "height" of a triangle? What does it measure? What is the "base"? Where is it located?

- If you opened a letter envelope out flat, unsealing all the seams, what part of the entire envelope is the back triangular flap?

_____

## Focus Question...

- Do you see any triangle shapes in this room? Are any of them part of a rectangle? If so, what part? What part of the rectangle would be left if the triangle were removed?

_____

## Problem...

Mari has an 8 x 10 sheet of paper. She needs to make a triangle by cutting from the lower left corner to the midpoint of the top side. What percent of the paper would she have left after she cut out the triangle? Mark your answer on the graph below.

### Percent of Paper Left After Cutting

| | |
|---|---|
| 0%–10% | |
| 11%–20% | |
| 21%–30% | |
| 31%–40% | |
| 41%–50% | |
| 51%–60% | |
| 61%–70% | |
| 71%–80% | |
| 81%–90% | |
| 91%–100% | |

# CUTTING AWAY A TRIANGLE

## Objectives
- to understand and apply ratios, proportions, and percents in a wide variety of situations
- to investigate relationships among fractions, decimals, and percents
- to visualize and represent geometric figures with special attention to spatial sense

## Materials
Graph paper, pencil, and scissors for each student

## Graphing
Give each student a sheet of graph paper. Ask them to draw a rectangle on the paper and count the total number of squares to find the area. (It makes no difference what size it is.) Have each student then cut a triangle from the lower left corner of their rectangle to the midpoint of the top side. Ask them to find the area of their triangle (by counting the total number of squares in the triangle) and to list the two areas they found on the chalkboard.

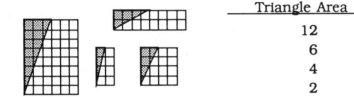

| Triangle Area | Rectangle Area |
|:---:|:---:|
| 12 | 48 |
| 6 | 24 |
| 4 | 16 |
| 2 | 8 |

## Discussing
When the students complete their data on areas, ask them to find the percent of the original rectangle that is left. Are they surprised? (Each should have 75% of the paper remaining. If anyone does not, stop to demonstrate.)

Now return to the original problem. Demonstrate how the 8 x 10 rectangle can be divided into four congruent triangles showing four equal pieces when they are flipped and rotated. Three out of four equal pieces is 75%.

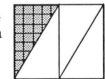

## Mathing
How might students find the area of the whole sheet of paper? Some will multiply length by width (10 × 8 = 80 square units). Others will connect the horizontal and vertical dots to complete 80 squares, then count or add. Can they count the squares in the triangle? (Some squares have been "cut" and need to be added to others to form whole squares.)

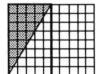

The total number of squares in the triangle is 20, and

$$80 - 20 = \mathbf{60} \text{ squares remaining.}$$

The problem then turns to what percent 60 is of 80. As a ratio, $^{60}/_{80}$ can be reduced to $^{3}/_{4}$, which can also be changed to $^{75}/_{100}$ or 75%.

## Answering
Since 75% of the paper is left, the range 71%–80% should be marked on the graph. Can the students determine what percent of the class marked the correct range?

## Extending
Divide a rectangle by cutting from the lower left corner to a point that is one-fourth of the way along the top side, then try one-eighth and one-sixteenth. Is there a pattern in the percentage that is left each time?

# ROLLING A CAN

**Initial Graph...**
Have you ever played the game "Kick the Can"? Circle your response below.

**Yes**          **No**          **I don't know**

_____

**Speaking of Games and Cans...**
- Where do you think the game of "Kick the Can" came from? Did some professional game-developer think of it or did it grow from other games? What makes you think so?
- Of what are cans made? Are they all made of the same material? Have they changed over the years? If so, how and why?
- What other games can you think of that use objects commonly found around the house? Do these games have rules? Are the rules the same everywhere the game is played? If not, how and why might they be different?

_____

**Focus Question...**
- Must "Kick the Can" be played with a perfectly-shaped, new can? Why or why not? Which rolls better, a round can or a "squished" can? How does the surface the can is kicked along affect its rolling speed or direction? For example, how would it roll on a bumpy surface? A smooth surface? A flat surface? A tilted surface?

_____

**Problem...**
If Genevieve rolls a soft drink can across her student desk, how many times do you think it will go around before it reaches the other side of the desk?

| # of Rolls | |
|:---:|---|
| 1 | |
| 2 | |
| 3 | |
| 4 | |
| 5 | |
| 6 | |
| 7 | |
| 8 | |
| 9 | |
| > 10 | |

# ROLLING A CAN

## Objective
- to represent and solve problems using geometric models
- to explore transformations of geometric figures

## Materials
One soft-drink can, a one-foot length of string, and a ruler or metric measure measure

## Demonstrating
Place a string around the soft-drink can and mark a circumference length with a colored marker. Remove the string and dangle it beside the height of the can for comparison. (Students are generally amazed that the circumference measurement of the can is greater than the height of the can.)

## Mathing
This problem is intended to get students to estimate the circumference of a can. Although the class may or may no be familiar with mathematical equations for the circumference of a circle, the problem is deliberately stated so as not to include the word "circumference." Let each student estimate the necessary number of rolls, then find the class **average** for those estimates. (The average is generally quite high, as many estimates are based on visualizing the cans lined up across the desk.)

## Discussing
A soft-drink can was chosen because most students are quite familiar with one and can visualize the size readily. This familiarity is important, as it makes the deviation of the estimates from the actual answer dramatic. Encourage the students to use critical and creative thinking to solve the problem and to think of various approaches. Seeing the circumference as a linear length provides an introduction of the fact that the circumference of every circle is a little more than three times the diameter of that same circle. To graph these relationships, see the **Extending** section below.

## Answering
An average of three rolls is needed for a soft-drink can to cross a student desk, assuming the desk is two feet wide.

## Extending
- Encourage students to estimate, then measure, how many times the can will go around as it rolls across various objects (i.e., the table, the window, the chalkboard, the room).
- Can they use these measurements to estimate how many times the can would go around if it rolled a much longer distance, such as down the hallway, across the playground, or around the school building?
- Ask each student to use the demonstrated string-measuring method to determine the circumference-to-height ratio of several various cans. If they graph the results, can they see any pattern? (Make sure that available cylinders are of a wide variety of heights and shapes.) Ask them to compare their circumference measurements with the distance across the widest part of the top of the same can. Is there any pattern to this ratio?

# GRAPHING INITIALS

**Problem...**

Martina Korvus, who is often called "Tinie" by her friends, found and marked the location of her initials on the graph below. First she found the M (for Martina) in the the bottom row, then she found the K (for Korvus) in the left column. She extended the M column and K row until they met, then placed an **X** at this spot for her name.

Can you graph your own initials in a similar fashion? Use only one **X** to represent your name.

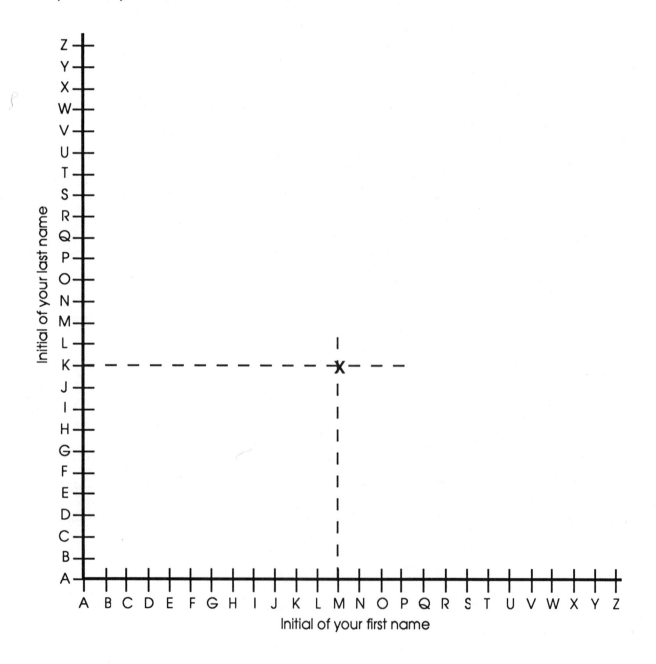

# GRAPHING INITIALS

## Objectives
- to systematically collect, organize, and describe data
- to construct, read, and interpret tables, charts, and graphs
- to make inferences and convincing arguments that are based on data analysis
- to develop an appreciation for statistical methods as a powerful means for decision making

## Graphing
This is a wonderful problem for introducing coordinates for two dimensions. Notice that the **first** value is the initial of the **first name** on the **horizontal axis** and that the **second** value is the initial of the **last name** on the **vertical axis**. It is important to relate which coordinate comes first by accepted standards. Have students label and discuss their coordinates. If duplicate initials occur, draw a "ring" around the X at the intersection of the row and column for each duplicate (see **Extending**, below).

## Discussing
Students are always interested in comparing their own response with those of the group.
- Where are the majority of answers? Where do they fall in relation to the frame of the graph?
- Where are there no responses?
- What coordinates would you expect to have few responses in the entire school?
- Are there any duplicates?
- The way of writing the coordinate for MARTINA KORVUS is (M,K). What if the name of someone in Martina's class was Kevin Matteson? Would his coordinate be the same as Martina's? How would it be labeled? (K,M) What coordinates repeat within this class? Do any coordinates match those of a famous person?

## Answering
Initial coordinates are marked on the graph to represent each individual student's name. The first coordinate (along the X axis) represents the initial of the first name, and the second coordinate (along the Y axis) represents the last name.

## Extending
Ask each student to predict the number of students in the whole school who might have the same initials. (It takes approximately 20 minutes to quickly make an entire graph of the whole school, dividing up class lists among several students and working on a large graph. It may be helpful to not put Xs on each initial, but rather to draw "stacked" rings—similar to "bulls' eyes"—around previous coordinates, even if they overlap.)

- How many students were "right-on" with their prediction of duplicate initials?
- Which initial was the most popular?
- Were earlier predictions of "nonresponse areas" correct?
- Would the most popular initial in your area be the most popular initial in other areas? In a survey of four schools, we found that "J" was the most popular first initial, but the most popular last initial varies. Why might this happen? Might this situation ever be reversed? If so, under what circumstances?

# ANGLE DEGREES

**Problem...**

Nellie loves to doodle. She has designed the angle drawn below as the newest basic symbol representing the simplicity of life. Can you estimate the number of degrees in this angle?

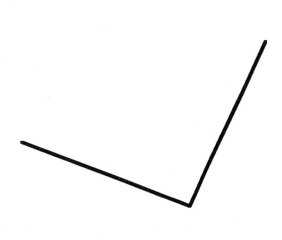

| # of degrees | |
|---|---|
| 0–10° | |
| 11–20° | |
| 21–30° | |
| 31–40° | |
| 41–50° | |
| 51–60° | |
| 61–70 ° | |
| 71–80 ° | |
| 81–90 ° | |
| 91–100° | |
| 101–110° | |
| 111–120° | |
| 121–130° | |
| 131–140° | |
| 141–150° | |
| 151–160° | |
| 161–170° | |
| > 170° | |

# ANGLE DEGREES

## Objectives
- to represent and solve problems using geometric models
- to visualize and represent geometric figures with special attention to developing spatial sense
- to understand the structure and use of systems of measurement

## Materials
Protractor (We recommend a clear protractor so measurements and method of measurement can be shown on the overhead transparency.)

## Graphing
Have each student put a mark on a class graph beside the number of degrees he or she estimates in the doodle. Ask the students what they could graph from the class data. What information could each graph be used to show?

## Discussing
Before doing any actual measurement, ask students how they made their estimate. Did they estimate the corner of a piece of paper to be 90° then estimate what was beyond? Did they start with a line representing 180° and estimate the part cut off? Did they have trouble with the way that the angle was turned or rotated in space? Comparison with a known is important. When you have measured the angle, ask how many students were in the right category on the graph. How did the estimates compare to the measurements?

## Demonstrating
It may be necessary to show students how to use a protractor to measure an angle. Measurement may be made using either ray as the base for the protractor, as shown here.

 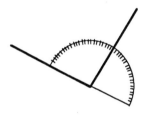

## Answering
The angle shown is 95 degrees.

## Extending
Distribute three construction-paper triangles with each angle labeled (1 through 9). Ask students to estimate the number of degrees in each angle. Next distribute protractors and ask the students to measure each angle to the nearest degree. Can they chart the data they gathered? How many degrees did each estimate vary from the actual measurement? What was the average difference?

| Angle # | Estimate ° | Actual ° | Difference |
|---------|-----------|----------|------------|
| 1 | 4 | 7 | 03 |
| 2 | 100 | 113 | 13 |
| 3 | 85 | 60 | 25 |
| 4 | 110 | 111 | 1 |
| 5 | 40 | 46 | 6 |
| 6 | 25 | 23 | 2 |
| 7 | 30 | 26 | 4 |
| 8 | 70 | 64 | 6 |
| 9 | 90 | 90 | 0 |
| TOTALS | 554 | 540 | 59 |

Average = 59 ÷ 9 = 7°

109

## PATHS

**Problem...**

Wallace wants to rent a movie tonight from a video store that is five blocks northeast of his home. He must walk a minimum of ten blocks from his house to the store along the sidewalks. How many different ten-block paths do you think he could take? Mark your response on the graph at the bottom of the page.

**Video Store**

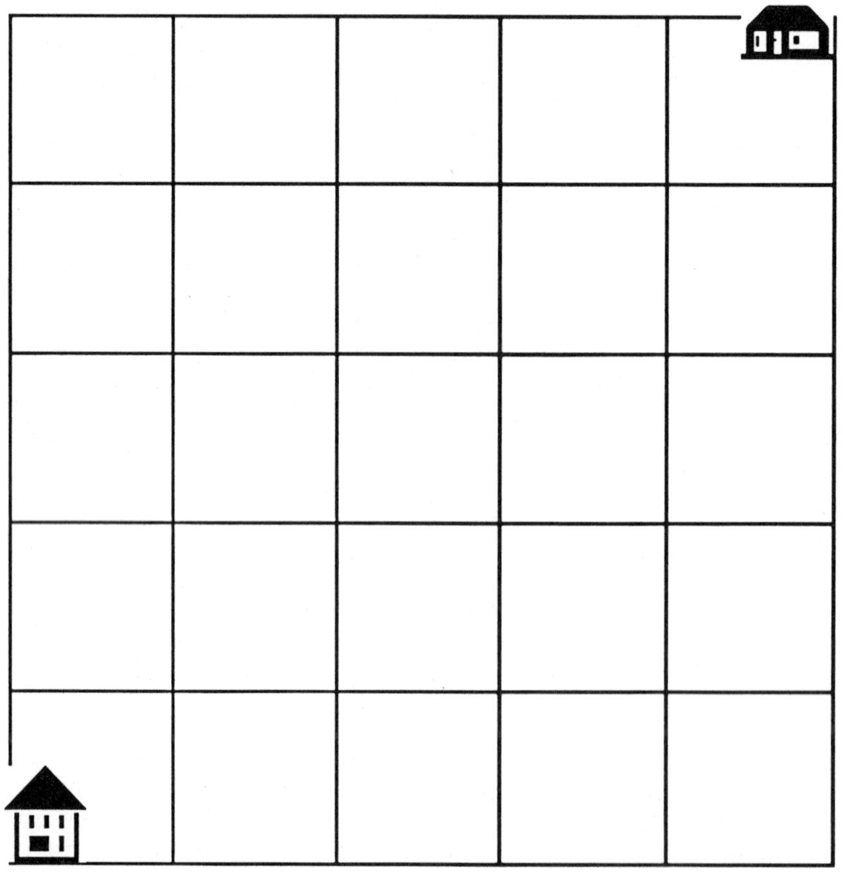

**Home**

| # of ways to walk to store | |
|---|---|
| 1–100 | |
| 101–200 | |
| 201–300 | |
| 301–400 | |
| 401–500 | |
| > 500 | |

# PATHS

## Objectives
- to describe, extend, analyze, and create a wide variety of patterns
- to appreciate the use and power of reasoning as a part of mathematics
- to model situations using oral, written, concrete, graphical, and algebraic methods

## Graphing

This problem emphasizes the importance of organizing data. Since that organization will take time, more than one period may be necessary to develop this lesson. For Wallace to jog to the video store in the minimum number of blocks, he cannot backtrack, thus he cannot jog to the south or west at any time.

Have students justify their answers. Some students may want to jump right into the 5 x 5 arrangement of blocks. But what if one begins with a 1 x 1 square, then a 2 x 2, and then continues? Would there be a pattern?

| Block Squares | Possible Paths | # of paths |
|---|---|---|
| 1 x 1 |  | 2 |
| 2 x 2 | 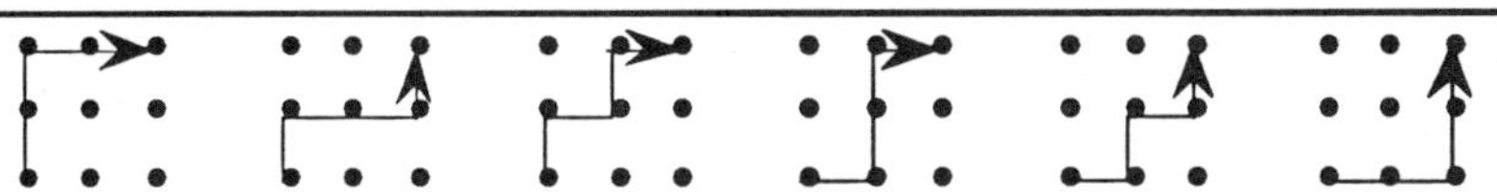 | 6 |
| 3 x 3 | 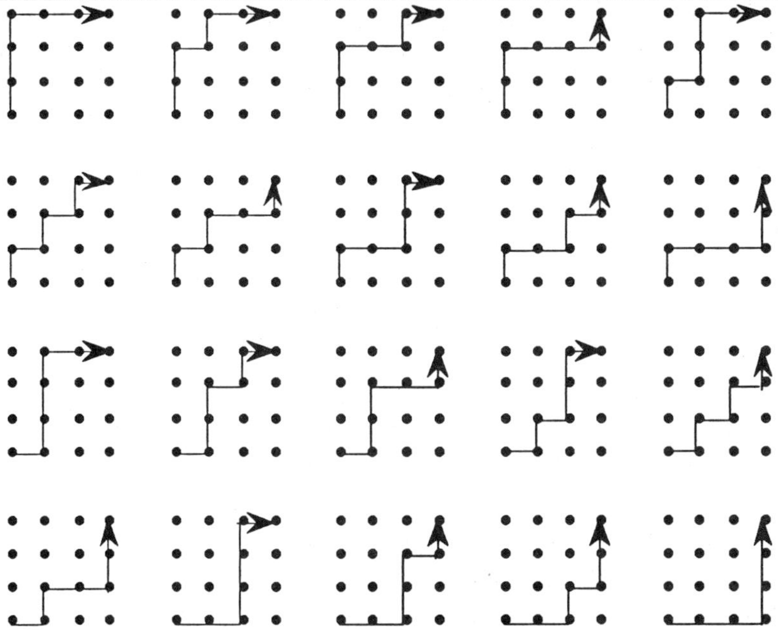 | 20 |

If students do not see any pattern yet, analysis at each point along the way might be in order. Reference to each corners can be made by **C(a,u)**; that is, the **Corner's location (Across, Up)** from home, as shown below.

|  |  |  | (Store) |
|---|---|---|---|
| C(0,3) | C(1,3) | C(2,3) | C(3,3) |
| C(0,2) | C(1,2) | C(2,2) | C(3,2) |
| C(0,1) | C(1,1) | C(2,1) | C(3,1) |
| C(0,0) | C(1,0) | C(2,0) | C(3,0) |
| (Home) | | | |

*[Continued on next page.]*

*[PATHS continued from previous page.]*

Students can then create a listing of all the different possible paths to each corner, similar to those shown on the grid below.

| From C(0,0) to: | Graphs of Possible Paths | Number |
|---|---|---|
| C(1,0) |  | 1 |
| C(0,1) |  | 1 |
| C(1,1) |  | 2 |
| C(2,0) |  | 1 |
| C(2,1) |  | 3 |
| C(2,2) | 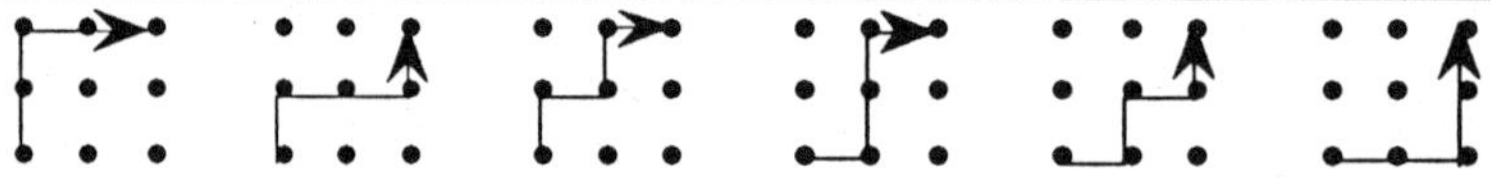 | 6 |
| C(1,2) |  | 3 |
| C(0,2) | 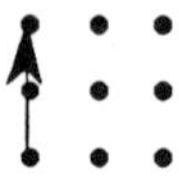 | 1 |
| C(3,0) | 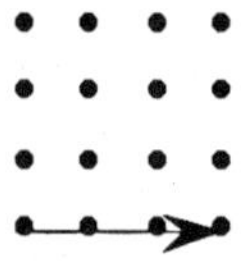 | 1 |
| C(3,1) | 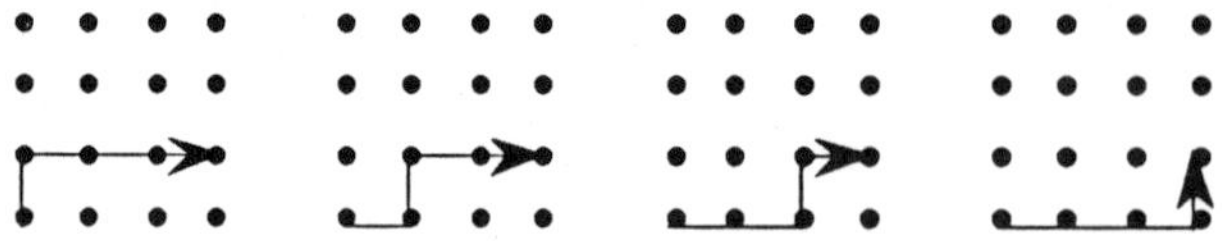 | 4 |
| C(3,2) | 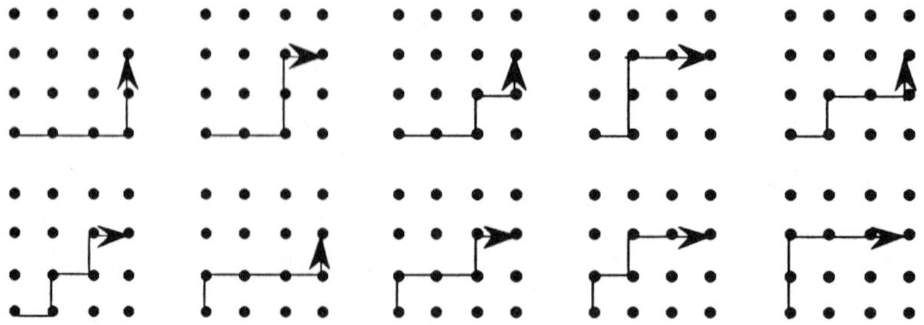 | 10 |

Extend the graph in the manner shown above for C(3,3), C(2,3), C(1,3), and C(0,3).

*[Continued on next page.]*

*[PATHS continued from previous page.]*

The number of possible paths between corners can then be placed at the exact grid coordinates using the following method.

|  |  |  |  | **(Store)** |
|---|---|---|---|---|
| 1 | • | • | • | • • • |
| 1 | • | • | • | • • • |
| 1 | 4 | 10 | 20 | • • • |
| 1 | 3 | 6 | 10 | • • • |
| 1 | 2 | 3 | 4 | • • • |
| 0 | 1 | 1 | 1 | • • • |

**(Home)**

Students should now be able to identify several patterns: the bottom row is all ones and the left column is all ones; all other numbers can be found by locating the number immediately below this "target" number and adding it to all numbers to its left—however many there are. For example, to find the "number" in the top row of the second column, one would add the number immediately below (5) to all numbers to the left of the 5. 5 + 1 = 6, which extends (or confirms) the pattern. This is a version of Pascal's Triangle.

Extending the above pattern to the 5 x 5 grid shown in the problem, then:

| 1 | 6 | 21 | 56 | 126 | 252 |
|---|---|---|---|---|---|
| 1 | 5 | 15 | 35 | 70 | 126 |
| 1 | 4 | 10 | 20 | 35 | 56 |
| 1 | 3 | 6 | 10 | 15 | 21 |
| 1 | 2 | 3 | 4 | 5 | 6 |
| 1 | 1 | 1 | 1 | 1 | 1 |

## Answering
There are 252 different paths which Wallace can take to the video store from his home.

## Extending
- What if there were particular sections where Wallace could not or did not want to walk? For example, if he did could not walk along the "sidewalks" of the shaded blocks shown below, what effect would that have on the number of possible routes that he could take to the store?

- What if it were possible for Wallace to retrace his steps occasionally? How would that affect the number of possible paths he could take to the store?

# GEOMETRIC BELT

### Initial Graph...

Are you wearing a belt today?  Mark your response on the graph below.

| Yes | No |
|-----|-----|
|     |    |

### Speaking of Belts...

- What part of the class is wearing belts today?
- Are certain types of belts more popular than others?  Are all belts detachable from the garment?  Are belts more popular with certain segments (classifications) of today's population?  If so, who?
- How many belts do you own?  What is the class average?  How many belts do you think are owned by the people in your family?  What is the average for your family?
- What did belts look like a hundred years ago?  What were they made of then?  What kind of materials are belts made of today?

### Focus Question...

- What is the function of a belt?  Can anything other than a belt be used to fulfill this function?  If so, name some things.  What designs have you see on belts?  Let's draw several.

### Problem...

This design is made of seven triangles.  Can you find them?

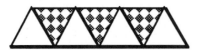

Chen has a belt made of 18 congruent triangles linked edge to edge similar to the design above.  If each triangular edge is one unit, what is the perimeter of his belt?

# GEOMETRIC BELT

## Objectives
- to understand and apply geometric properties and relationships
- to analyze functional relationships to explain how a change in one quantity results in a change in another
- to use patterns and functions to represent and solve problems
- to extend students' understanding of the concept of perimeter

## Graphing
Many students solve the problem of the perimeter of 18 triangles by drawing or building a model, which is an excellent means of reinforcing how "perimeter" is measured.

## Discussing
After several demonstrations using different numbers of triangles, ask the students if they think there might be a relationship between the number of triangles in this belt and its perimeter. What relationships do they see? How could they verify their ideas?

## Mathing
A table may be formed from several investigations:

| # triangles | 1 | 2 | 3 | 4 | 5 | 6 | 7 | ••• |
|---|---|---|---|---|---|---|---|---|
| perimeter | 3 | 4 | 5 | 6 | 7 | 8 | 9 | ••• |

Following this pattern, what would the perimeter be of a 100-triangle belt? Ask students to justify their solution. There are several possible methods, including:
- The first and last triangle have two edges on the perimeter and all other triangles one. A pattern is then formed for total perimeter.
$$2 + 1 + 1 + 1 + • • • + 1 + 1 + 2 = 102$$
- $100 \div 2 = 50$ top edges, 50 bottom edges, and one edge at each end.
$$50 + 50 + 1 + 1 = 102$$
- Ten smaller sections of ten triangles each could be linked. The perimeter of each ten-triangle group is 12, and 9 connecting links of two matching edges would be needed to join the groups into one 100-triangle belt.
$$(12 \times 10) - (9 \times 2) = 102$$
- The pattern from the table above reveals that the perimeter is always two more than the number of triangles in the belt.

## Answering
A belt of 18 congruent triangles placed edge to edge has a perimeter of 20 units.

## Extending
- What would the perimeter of the belt be if it were made of 17 one-unit squares? What about pentagons? Hexagons?
- What happens if the belt is made of polygons of two or more shapes—such as a pattern of two squares followed by one hexagon. If polygons are joined only along edges (see diagram below), and if each side of every polygon is one unit in length, what would the perimeter be for a 100-piece belt made of this pattern?

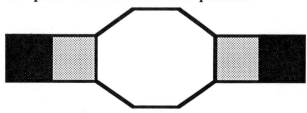

# THREE-SIDED BINS

**Initial Graph...**
What kinds of things do you collect?  Write the name of your favorite collection on the line below.

_____

**Speaking of Collections...**
- How long have you been collecting items for the collection you named?  How and why did you get started?  Why do you collect this kind of thing rather than other similar items?  Do other members of your family help you collect items?
- Can your collection be completed?  Do you have a goal set for completing it?  What do you plan to do with the collection?  Is it valuable?  Do you know what it is worth?  How can (or did) you find out?
- If you were to start a collection today, what would you like to collect?  Why?

_____

**Focus Question...**
- What do you use to store or keep your collection?  Why do you use this type of storage?  What other methods might you use?  What are the advantages and disadvantages of each?

_____

**Problem...**
Zita would like to build a bin to hold her rock collection.  Some of the rocks in her collection are large and heavy, so she needs a very strong bin.  Someone told her that a triangular-shaped bin with a post in each corner would be the strongest shape to use.

She has three long boards that can be cut to any length, and she has found nine sturdy posts sunk into the ground on a corner of her property.  If you use the diagram below to represent those posts, how many different sizes of triangular-shaped bins can you design for Zita to choose from?

# THREE-SIDED BINS

### Objectives
- to represent and solve problems using geometric models
- to identify, describe, compare, and classify geometric figures
- to visualize and represent geometric figures with special attention to developing spatial sense
- to develop an appreciation of geometry as a means of describing the physical world

### Materials
Peg- or geoboards, rubber bands, graph paper, and pencil for each student or group

### Graphing
Ask students to draw their triangles on graph paper using a "post" for each vertex.

### Mathing
This problem focuses on discovering noncongruent triangles on a 3 x 3 peg- or geoboard. The solution reinforces congruency and involves critical and creative thinking. The word *noncongruent* may stump a few students. It can quickly be demonstrated by creating several triangles of the same shape (*congruent*) on a geoboard. The following triangles, for example, would be counted as only one bin design.

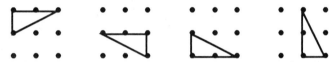

Students may come up with several ways of organizing their data. A diagram of possible triangles is shown below.

### Discussing
When students have completed their graphing, help them compare their triangles with those created by their classmates. Encourage them to talk about and compare the various attributes of the triangles, including area, perimeter, angle size, and length of sides.

### Answering
8 noncongruent triangular bins can be created, as the diagrams above illustrate.

### Extending
- If you wanted to give a proper geometric title to each triangle you used, how many would you label isosceles? Label each bin.
- What difference would it make if the triangular bins did not need a post in each corner but rather needed only to be supported twice—at any placement—along each side?

  **EXAMPLE:**

  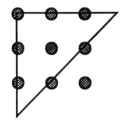

# THE PENDULUM SWINGS

### Initial Graph...
Which of the following words do you think refers to an object that swings back and forth at a regular rate? Circle your answer choice.

**Pendulum**          **Penguin**          **Petroleum**

---

### Speaking of Swings...
- If you were on a swing, what would make you swing higher above the ground? At what point of the swing's arc are you closest to the ground? Furthest away?
- How do you make a swing stop swinging? Can you stop it without touching the ground with your feet?
- Without sitting in the swing, can you make it stay "perfectly still" when you take your hands off it? Is it hard to do? Why or why not?
- A swing works like a pendulum. As a matter of fact, the scientist Galileo discovered the laws of the pendulum by watching the swing of a hanging lamp. What other objects can you think of that work like a pendulum?

---

### Focus Question...
- Do you think that the number of ropes have any affect on the speed of the swing? For example, do you swing faster on a swing with one chain or rope, like a tire swing, or on a swing with two chains or ropes, like a playground swing?

---

### Problem...
Jessica and Kemil have started a game that involves a pendulum. Kemil would like to win, so he needs to find out a little bit about pendulums. He would like to know whether a pendulum swings faster on a shorter string or a longer string. What do **you** think? Mark your response on the graph below.

| a pendulum swings faster on a shorter string | |
|---|---|
| a pendulum swings faster on a longer string | |
| a pendulum swings at the same rate, no matter what length the string is | |

# THE PENDULUM SWINGS

## Objectives
- to develop an appreciation of geometry as a means of describing the physical world
- to analyze functional relationships to explain how a change in one quantity results in a change in another
- to describe and represent relationships with tables, graphs, and rules
- to develop and apply number-theory concepts (e.g., primes, factors, multiples) in real-world and mathematical problem situations

## Discussing
Ask students to explain their choices, then have groups of students perform the task by placing a weight (washers work wonderfully) on a string. Have them vary the length of the string as it hangs over the edge a desk. Everyone should observe the same results. (If anyone does not, stop and have that student demonstrate for you.)

## Answering
The shorter the string, the faster the pendulum swings.

## Extending
- Make a two-dimensional graph for a pendulum with varying lengths of the string. Record the time in seconds for ten swings. Is the graph a linear equation? Can students find the equation that represents this graph given the linear distance on the string (Y) and the time for ten swings (X)?

|   | | | | | | | | | | | | | |
|---|---|---|---|---|---|---|---|---|---|---|---|---|---|
| **18** | | | | | | | | | | | | | |
| **15** | | | | | | | | | | | | | |
| **12** | | | | | | | | | | | | | |
| **9** | | | | | | | | | | | | | |
| **6** | | | | | | | | | | | | | |
| **3** | | | | | | | | | | | | | |

Length of string (inches)

2   4   6   8   10   12   14   16   18   20   22   24   26

Time for ten swings (seconds)

- Vary the pendulum weight. (The period of a pendulum is dependent upon the length of the string and does not vary by a change in pendulum weight. Graphing *time* versus *weight* results in a line parallel to the weight axis.)
- Vary the distance from the vertical rest position before release. (Again, there should be no difference in the speed of a pendulum due to vertical release.)

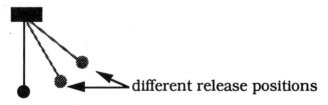

different release positions

# STRETCH

**Initial Graph...**
Stretch your hand open as far as you can. What do you think the distance is between the tip of your thumb and the tip of your little finger? Mark your response (in inches) with an **X** on the graph below.

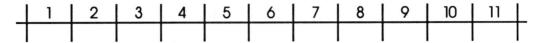

**Speaking of Stretching...**
- Measure the distance you estimated above. Mark the measurement with a √ on the graph above. How does your estimate compare to the actual measurement? What is the average handspan (stretch) in the class? What would that be in metric measurement?

- If you stand on one foot, how far can you stretch the other foot away from your body? How far can you stretch your smile from corner to corner?

**Focus Question...**
- How tall are you in inches? If we arrange ourselves by heights, tallest to shortest, would our hand stretch distances also be in sequence?

**Problem...**
We have two yard sticks taped to the wall so they measure a straight line six feet long. You may use them to measure the distance you are able to stretch your arms apart (from finger tip to finger tip). Mark your answer on the graph below by placing one **X** that is in the row of your height (in inches) and in the column of your stretch (in inches). Extend the graph if you need to.

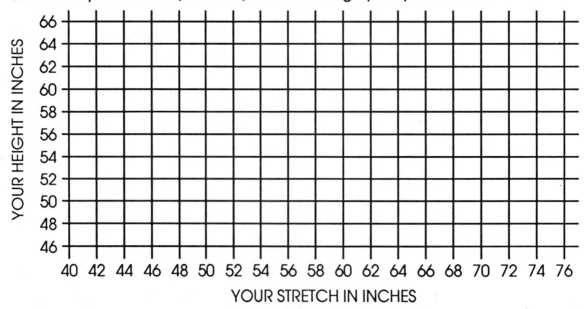

YOUR STRETCH IN INCHES

# STRETCH

## Objectives
- to understand the structure and use of systems of measurement
- to estimate, make, and use measurements to describe and compare phenomena
- to evaluate arguments that are based on data analysis
- to develop an appreciation of geometry as a means of describing the physical world

## Materials
Two yard- or meter sticks taped horizontally along the wall at a height that students can easily reach. You may also need to use these to measure student height.

## Graphing
The purpose of this problem is for the student to compare measured height with stretch. (This can be done in metric units as well as inches.) Since each student places a mark on the two-dimensional graph comparing height and stretch, two linear measurements are needed. The result should approximate a straight diagonal line, as shown below.

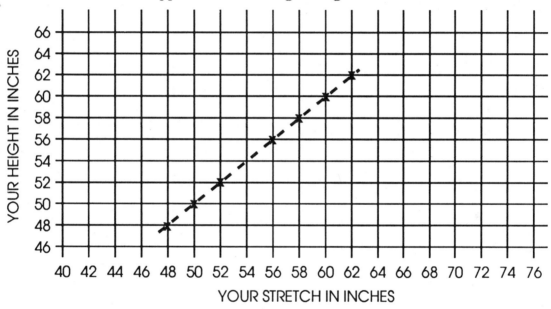

## Discussing
Ask several students to demonstrate how they measured their stretch and placed their mark on the class graph. Did everyone in the class use the same procedure? (If not, have the class agree on how stretch and height are measured, then remeasure.) Ask students to draw statistical information from the chart. What is the average class height? What is the mode (most frequent)? What could be said about the average comparison between a student's height and stretch? (equal) Draw a picture of a person with a large deviation from the norm. Can you draw a picture of a person with an opposite deviation from the one you first drew?

## Answering
The average person has an arm stretch equal to his or her own height.

## Extending
How does the stretch on one hand between the tip of your thumb and the tip of your small finger (handspan) compare with the length of your hand from the wrist to the tip of the middle finger? How does the length of your foot compare to the length of your leg? Make a ratio of these measurements. How does this ratio compare to the handspan-hand length and the armspan-height ratios?

# FOOT LENGTH

**Problem...**

Podie has noticed that some people seem to have small feet. He wonders if there is some relationship between how tall people are and the size of their feet. Can you help him get some information?

Measure your height in centimeters, then measure the length of your foot (from heel to toe) in centimeters. Place one **X** on the graph that is in the row of your foot measurement and the column of your height measurement.

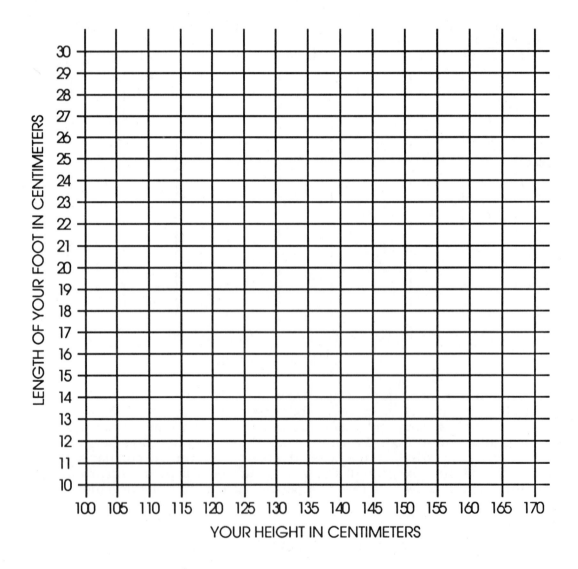

LENGTH OF YOUR FOOT IN CENTIMETERS

YOUR HEIGHT IN CENTIMETERS

# FOOT LENGTH

## Objectives
- to estimate, make, and use measurements to describe and compare phenomena
- to extend students' understanding of the process of measurement
- to select appropriate units and tools for measuring to the degree of accuracy required in a particular situation
- to understand the structure and use of systems of measurement
- to develop the concepts of rates and other derived and indirect measurements

## Materials
Metric measurement materials (Note: Metric measure is used for greater measurement variation. You might also use this problem to compare inches and feet to metric units.)

## Demonstration
Students may need a demonstration of measuring for height (without shoes is best) and length of feet (again, without shoes). It may be necessary to use teams, with each taking a turn placing a ruler on the other's head, perpendicular to the wall, to get a height measurement. Did every student measure correctly? How could accuracy of measurements be checked?

## Graphing
Once the class is satisfied with their individual measurements and their mark's placement on the class graph, concentrate on the pattern indicated by the responses. Do they appear to go in a straight line? What does that tell you about the relationship between human feet and height? Draw a line that approximates the middle range of the two variables.

## Mathing
What is the average height of the students in the class? What is the average foot length? Find the line that best fits the center of the marks on your graph. Where would the mark indicating this "average" person fall in relation to this line?

## Answering
The following example of a class graph shows the established linear measurement.

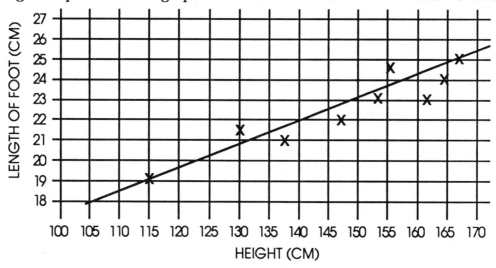

## Extending
- If each person divided his or her height in centimeters by the number of centimeters of his or her own foot length and carried the answer out to the nearest hundredth place, how close would all the answers be?
- Once a relationship has been established and a line agreed upon, ask students to estimate the height of a giant whose footprint measures 60 centimeters in length!

# HEIGHT OF THE ROOM

## Initial Graph...

How far is it from the furthest wall of the classroom to the front of the teacher's desk? Write your estimate at the arrow on the number line below, then add to the number line by putting appropriate numbers in the boxes on each side of the arrow.

## Speaking of Judging Distance...

- What unit of measure did you use to estimate your answer to the **Initial Graph**? How many different units that measure distance can you think of? If you had used a different one, how would it affect the other numbers you put on the number line?

- Great distances, like those between stars and planets, are measured in "light years." How far do you think "one light year" is? Could you find out?

- What is the smallest unit you can think of that measures distance between objects? What kinds of distances might need to be measured in very tiny units? What type of job might demand that you accurately measure something minute?

## Focus Question...

- If you open a book on your desk and sit up straight, how far do you think it is from your eyes to the book? If you look out the classroom window, what is the most distant object that you can see? How far away do you think it is? Which of these two distances was easier to estimate? Which estimate do you think is closer to the actual measurement?

## Problem...

To the nearest foot, estimate how far it is from the floor to the ceiling in your classroom. On the graph below, place an **X** to the right of your estimate.

### Ceiling height in feet

| <6 | | 9 | | 13 | | 17 | |
|----|---|----|---|----|---|-----|---|
| 6  | | 10 | | 14 | | 18 | |
| 7  | | 11 | | 15 | | 19 | |
| 8  | | 12 | | 16 | | >19 | |

# HEIGHT OF THE ROOM

## Objectives
- to understand the structure and use of systems of measurement
- to extend students' understanding of the process of measurement
- to select appropriate units and tools for measuring to the degree of accuracy required in a particular situation

## Materials
Ruler, yard-, or meter stick

## Mathing
Ask the students to find the class average for the estimated height of the room. Ask each how his or her original estimate compares with the class average.

## Graphing
Students may use a bar graph for comparing individual estimates with the measured height.

## Discussing
(Note: This problem may be pursued using either English or Metric measurements, at your discretion.) Ask individual students how they arrived at an estimate. Some students may say that they estimated how many students, standing one on top of the other, would stack to the ceiling. Others may try to mentally mark off units until they reach the ceiling. Some will estimate the chalkboard height and compare it with the remaining wall below and above, adding all three estimations. I had one student try to divide the height into two sections, then divide again and estimate the feet in the section remaining to multiply by four for the final result. Students may also refer to objects of known height outside the room as a basis of comparison. Some may even know the average height of doors and compare this with the distance over the door. However students may justify their answers, it is important to listen to as many as possible so that other students will gain several insights into attacking problems similar to this.

The actual height of the room can be measured with many various lengths. You may use a yard- or meter stick and put marks on the wall at specific intervals up from the floor (a foot or a yard or a meter), then stop and ask for new estimates. Most students think that equal measurements are actually longer on the upper section of the wall. The angle at which students perceive the wall may vary the estimated heights.

## Answering
The average classroom is 12 feet in height, but answers may vary.

## Extending
Estimate the dimensions of the classroom floor, then mark the estimations on a two-dimensional graph.

# NAIL WEIGHT

### Initial Graph...
On the desk you will see a balance and a nail. In ounces, how much do you think that nail weighs? Mark your response on the number-line graph below.

0  1  2  3  4  5  6  7  8  9  10  11  12  13

### Speaking of Nails...
- What would this same nail weigh in grams? What objects in this room weigh about the same as this nail? What weighs less? What weighs about double?
- Who first invented nails? What did the first nails look like? What were they used for? What materials were they made of? Are they still made of the same material today?

### Focus Question...
- In what kind of a store could you get nails? How are they sold? Can you buy different types of nails for different uses? Do all nails weigh the same?

### Problem...
Wade has put some scales and some sacks on the table. Each sack has a different number of nails. Choose a bag of nails and weigh it. Then count the number of nails, and place one **X** on the graph below to show the row for the number of nails in the bag and the column for the weight you found.

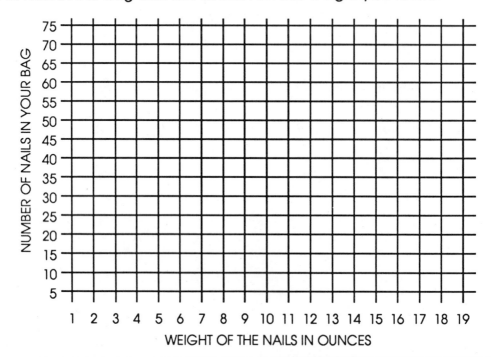

NUMBER OF NAILS IN YOUR BAG

WEIGHT OF THE NAILS IN OUNCES

# NAIL WEIGHT

## Objectives
- to extend students' understanding of the concepts of weight and mass
- to understand the structure and use of systems of measurement
- to extend students' understanding of the process of measurement
- to estimate, make, and use measurements to describe and compare phenomena
- to systematically collect, organize, and describe data

## Materials
Scales (preferably several different types) and a small bag of nails for each student or group of students. Be sure that all the nails are the same type (i.e. 16 penny,...)

## Demonstrating
Ask students to demonstrate how they found the weight per bag using the various types of scales available. When all students are satisfied that they have correctly weighed their bag, counted the nails, and placed their response on the classroom graph, focus their attention on the total responses for the class.

## Graphing
Do the majority of the responses appear to be in a straight line? (They certainly should, since the weight of each nail is approximately the same as every other nail.) Establish a line that approximates this relationship.

## Mathing
Ask students to use the weight of the bag of nails to find the weight of a single nail. (You may need to remind them that the bag weighs something, too.) If you have access to scales that can measure small weights, students may wish to check their computation by actually weighing a single nail.

## Answering
The class graph should result in a straight line whose slope is the number of nails per ounce.

## Extending
- What would the projected weight be for 1200 nails of this size?
- Weigh sealed bags of the same type of nails. From the weights, determine how many nails are inside each bag? Open the bag and count the nails to determine how far off the answers were.

---

# ROCK VOLUME

**Problem...**
Geo found the rock in the front of the room on his last rock-hunting trip. He would like to know the volume of the rock. How many cubic inches do you think the rock has? Put your name beside your estimate.

**Cubic Inches**

| | |
|---|---|
| > 15 | |
| 15 | |
| 14 | |
| 13 | |
| 12 | |
| 11 | |
| 10 | |
| 9 | |
| 8 | |
| 7 | |
| 6 | |
| 5 | |
| 4 | |
| 3 | |
| 2 | |
| 1 | |

# ROCK VOLUME

## Objectives
- to extend students' understanding of the process of measurement
- to estimate, make, and use measurements to describe and compare phenomena
- to select appropriate units and tools for measuring to the degree of accuracy required in a particular situation
- to understand the structure and use of systems of measurement
- to extend students' understanding of the concepts of volume, weight and mass
- to develop the concepts of rates and other derived and indirect measurements
- to introduce the concept of "specific gravity" (**Extending** Activity)

## Materials
A rock for the students to measure (You might place a ruler beside the rock on the table so that estimates for volume might be calculated with actual linear measurements.)

## Discussing
Ask each student to explain how he or she arrived at an estimate. Some students may find the longest distance on the rock and the shortest distance on the rock and then multiply. You may need to remind them that three measurement values are necessary to find volume. Some students will take each of the three measurements at the maximum height, width, or length. That would also be incorrect, as the rock does not take that maximum volume but an average.

## Mathing
Ask students how they might find a more accurate volume than the estimate above. Hopefully, someone will suggest the volume the rock will displace when placed in a container with water.

A gallon of water contains 231 cubic inches. Since there are 16 cups in a gallon, that makes $231/16$, or approximately 14.4 cubic inches per cup.

Fill a large measuring container (at least eight-cup capacity) to the four-cup mark and place the rock in the container. (If part of the rock remains out of the water, use a larger measuring device and additional water.) Ask students to note the difference in water level that results from the rock being placed in the container. Subtracting the original four cups from the new level results in the displacement of the rock itself. Since each cup displaces 14.4 cubic inches, the total number of cups displaced by the volume of the rock can be multiplied by 14.4 for the volume in cubic inches. (This procedure may be simplified if measuring devices are available in cubic inches or cubic centimeters.)

## Answering
To estimate the volume of a rock, find three directions for the rock, estimate an average height, width, and length in inches, then multiply the three numbers to find an estimated volume. For a more accurate estimate, the volume of the rock is taken as the displaced volume when that rock is placed in water.

## Extending
Rock hounds are often interested in the specific gravity of individual rocks, as that helps them identify rocks and minerals by name. "Specific gravity" is found by dividing the volume of a rock by its weight. What is the specific gravity for the rock used in the problem above?

# PERIMETERS WITH A CONSTANT AREA

**Problem...**

Kim has a sheet with dots that are one unit apart. She has been trying use squares joined along edges to draw different figures that have an *area = 5 units.* One of the figures Kim has drawn is shown below.

How many other figures can you draw that have different shapes but still are made of squares and have an area of five units?

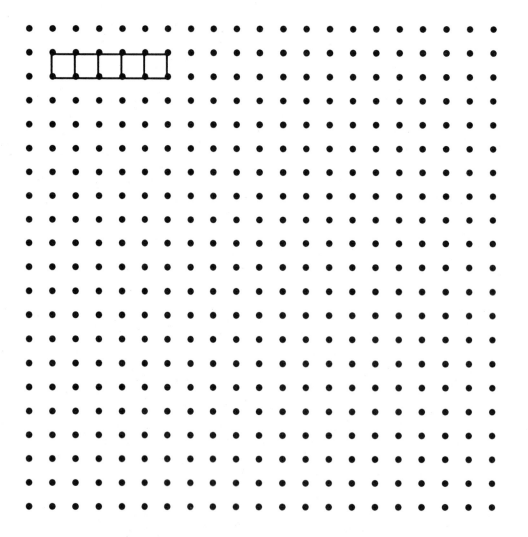

# PERIMETERS WITH A CONSTANT AREA

## Objectives
- to extend students' understanding of the concepts of perimeter and area
- to analyze functional relationships to explain how a change in one quantity results in a change in another
- to explore problems and describe results using graphical, numerical, physical, algebraic, and verbal mathematical models or representations
- to develop the concepts of rates and other derived and indirect measurements

## Mathing
Ask students to identify the **noncongruent** figures (those that cannot be rotated or flipped in space to make the others). Can they think of others? (There are ten; see below.) Ask them to compare the perimeters of the figures they have chosen. Are all the perimeters equal? Have the students write the perimeter of each figure below their diagrams, as shown below (A = area; P = perimeter).

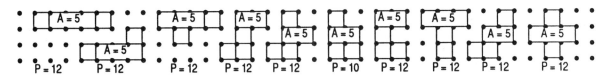

## Discussing
*"Do you notice anything special about the figure with area 5 and perimeter 10? Why do you think it's different? Check your theories by using figures drawn in a similar manner but with **area = 4**."*

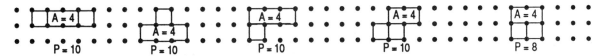

By now, students may have noted similarities for figures with a constant area but various perimeters. They will easily catch on if you ask them to circle any **DOTS** on the interior of each figure. One dot on the inside lowers the perimeter by two.

## Answering
There are ten noncongruent figures with an area of five. Nine of them have a perimeter of 12, but the one shown to the right has a perimeter of ten.

## Extending
- What happens to the perimeter measurement if there are two dots on the interior of a figure?
- On the basis of what you have learned about interior dots, draw three different figures that have *area = 6*: one with a perimeter of 14, one with a perimeter of 12, and one with a perimeter of 10.

**Examples:**

# CIRCLE AND SQUARE

**Problem...**
Niki has used a string of known length to draw the circle and the square below. Each shape has the same perimeter (distance around the outside). Do you think one has a larger area than the other? Mark your response on the graph below the shapes.

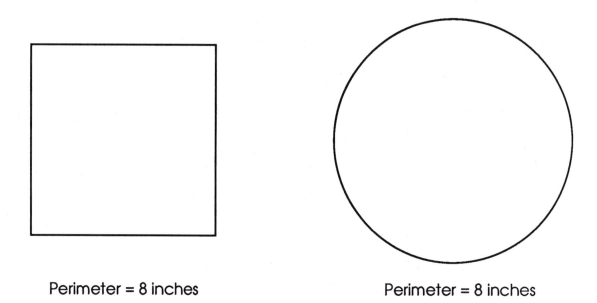

Perimeter = 8 inches          Perimeter = 8 inches

## Which shape has a larger area?

| The circle | The square | Neither |
|------------|------------|---------|
|            |            |         |
|            |            |         |
|            |            |         |

# CIRCLE AND SQUARE

## Objectives
- to extend students' understanding of the concepts of perimeter and area
- to select appropriate units and tools for measuring to the degree of accuracy required in a particular situation
- to extend students' understanding of the process of measurement
- to visualize and represent geometric figures with attention to developing spatial sense
- to understand and apply geometric properties and relationships

## Materials
Graph paper and knotted string (see below)

## Demonstrating
Divide the class into groups. You will need at least two people per group, as it takes four hands to move the string around adequately for this problem. Give each group two sheets of graph paper and a string. Use strings with knots tied to indicate varying lengths (4", 8", 12", 16", 20", 24", 28", ...). Ask students to work as a team to make a circle on one sheet of graph paper, a square of the same perimeter on the other, mark the outline of each with a pencil, and count the number of squares inside the figure.

## Mathing
Have each group list their area counts on the chalkboard; for example:

| Group | String Loop | Area of the Square | Area of the Circle |
|-------|-------------|--------------------|--------------------|
| 1 | 4" | 1 | 1 |
| 2 | 8" | 4 | 5 |
| 3 | 12" | 9 | 11.5 |
| 4 | 16" | 16 | 20 |
| 5 | 20" | 25 | 32 |
| 6 | 24" | 36 | 46 |
| 7 | 28" | 49 | 62 |

Do the students notice a pattern? (The difference between the two areas appears to increase as the string loop increases.)

## Graphing
Students may plot the area-perimeter ratio of the squares from the above chart on a two-dimensional graph and connect the plotted points with a diagonal line. Ask them to plot the area-perimeter ratio of the circles on the same graph using a different color. What general pattern do they notice about the distance between the plotted lines?

## Answering
The circle has the larger area.

## Extending
Find the mathematical relationship for the area of a square and circle formed with a perimeter of length $x$:

Answer: The area of a square with perimeter $x$ is equal to $\frac{x^2}{16}$.

The area of a circle with perimeter $x$ is equal to $\frac{x^2}{4\pi}$.

# TRIANGLE COUNT

### Initial Graph...
How many triangles do you see in this figure? Count them and mark your response on the graph below.

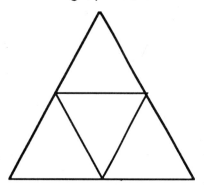

1
2
3
4
5
6
7
8
9

### Speaking of Triangles...
- Use a different color to trace each triangle in the figure above. What kind of triangles are they? How many different sizes of triangles are there? How many of each size?
- Do you see any objects or shapes in this room that are made of triangles? Is there anything that is made up of more than five triangles?
- If you look at the above figure as a pattern and extend that pattern one more row, how many triangles would the new figure contain?

### Problem...
Thom has spent a long time counting the possible combinations that make triangles of all sizes in the figure below. Help him by making your own count.

| # of triangles | |
|---|---|
| 1–10 | |
| 11–20 | |
| 21–30 | |
| 31–40 | |
| 41–50 | |
| 51–60 | |
| 61–70 | |
| 71–80 | |
| 81–90 | |
| 91–100 | |
| more than 100 | |

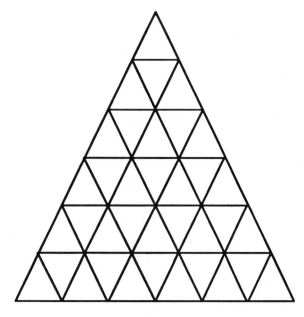

# TRIANGLE COUNT

## Objectives
- to describe, extend, analyze, and create a wide variety of patterns
- to use patterns and functions to represent and solve problems
- to explore transformations of geometric figures

## Discussing
Ask students how they organized their count. Did they notice that some triangles pointed upward and some downward? Did they notice that certain triangles overlap others? Did they see triangles of different sizes?

point upward

... downward

## Graphing
Ask students to count only the triangles that "point upward." (Triangles that "point upward" will range in area from 1 to 36, as follows.)

| Area (units) | No. of triangles | Counted triangles (shown) |
|---|---|---|
| 1 | 1 + 2 + 3 + 4 + 5 + 6 | |
| 4 | 1 + 2 + 3 + 4 + 5 | |
| 9 | 1 + 2 + 3 + 4 | ...  ...  ...  ... |
| 16 | 1 + 2 + 3 | ...  ...  ... |
| 25 | 1 + 2 | ...  ... |
| 36 | 1 | ... |

Next, ask students to consider only those triangles that "point downward." (From smallest to largest, area will range from 1 to 9.)

| Area = 1 | 1 + 2 + 3 + 4 + 5 | |
|---|---|---|
| Area = 4 | 1 + 2 + 3 | ...  ... |
| Area = 9 | 1 | ... |

## Mathing
The total number of triangles can be found by adding the numbers in the second column above for both the upward and downward triangles.

## Answering
The correct range would be 71–80 triangles in the figure; the exact count is 78.

## Extending
How many triangles would be found in a similar figure with 20, instead of 6, small triangles at the base? Is it still possible to find the answer by dividing the triangles into two groups?

# THE AREA ON A PAINTED CUBE

## Initial Graph...
What do you know about a cube? Shade the area on the diagram that shows your response.

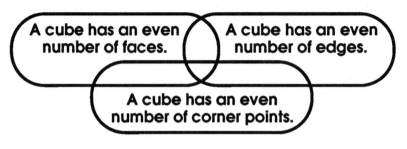

## Speaking of Cubes...
- Where are the faces, edges, and corner points on a cube? Can you point to them on a sugar cube? If you were to paint all the faces of a sugar cube with food coloring, how many faces would you paint?
- Do you see anything in this room that is a cube? How many faces do you see? What colors are they? Describe the shape of each face.
- What cubical items can you buy in a grocery store? Why are many boxes cubical? If a basketball comes in a cubical box, what space is wasted?
- What does it look like on the inside of a cube? Describe each "face" on the cubical head of a robot.

## Focus Question...
- If you sliced a wooden cube into three equal sections using horizontal cuts, how many cuts would you have to make? What shape would each "slice" be? How many faces would each individual slice have?

## Problem...
Trina painted the outside of this wooden cube with jet-black paint. Then she sliced it twice in each direction, as shown below. This broke the original cube up into 27 smaller cubes. How many of these new, smaller cubes have:

3 sides of black paint _____

2 sides of black paint _____

1 side of black paint _____

0 sides of black paint _____

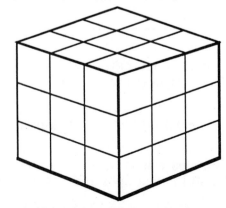

# THE AREA ON A PAINTED CUBE

## Objectives
- to represent and solve problems using geometric models
- to visualize and represent geometric figures with attention to developing spatial sense
- to analyze functional relationships to explain how a change in one quantity results in a change in another
- to develop and apply number-theory concepts (e.g., primes, factors, multiples) in real-world and mathematical problem situations

## Demonstrating
Assume that each side of all units after the cuts will = 1. Therefore, the original larger cube would be considered 3 x 3 x 3. Have an object ready for demonstration. A large cube constructed of 27 interlocking cubes works well. Wrap this larger cube with black electrical tape, covering the entire outside surface. The 27 individual cubes can then be carefully cut apart with a razor blade to justify student answers.

## Answering
The number of new cubes with similarly colored surface area are shown below.

 3 faces black = 8
(one in each corner)

 2 faces black = 12
(four on each face joining 2 faces)

 1 face black = 6
(one in center of each face)

 0 faces black = 1
(in the middle of the cube)

## Extending and Discussing
Ask students what they think will happen if they make more slices in the cube. (A pattern should form for the number of smaller cubes with 3, 2, 1, 0 sides black.) Attempt a 4 x 4 x 4 cube next, then a 5 x 5 x 5 cube, and so on. Ask the students to compare the counts and to explain how they vary for cubes with increasing numbers of slices. Eventually, students should see patterns for sections.

| Number of faces black ↓ | 2 x 2 x 2 cube | 3 x 3 x 3 cube | 4 x 4 x 4 cube | 5 x 5 x 5 cube | $n$ x $n$ x $n$ cube |
|---|---|---|---|---|---|
| 3 | 8 | 8 | 8 | 8 | 8 |
| 2 | 0 | 12 | 24 | 36 | $12(n-2)$ |
| 1 | 0 | 6 | 24 | 54 | $6(n-2)^2$ |
| 0 | 0 | 1 | 8 | 27 | $(n-2)^3$ |
| Total cubes → | 8 | 27 | 64 | 125 | $n^3$ |

## Graphing
Have the students plot the information from the above chart on two-dimensional graphs. Encourage them to discuss and compare their findings.

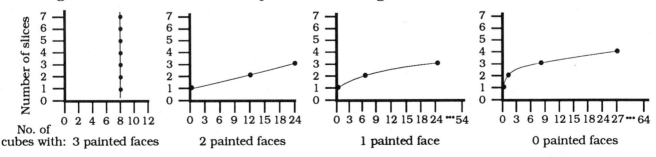

# VOLUME OF AN EGG

**Initial Graph...**
What kinds of foods do you prefer to eat for breakfast?  Mark the area on the diagram that indicates your response.

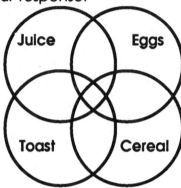

_____

**Speaking of Breakfast...**
- What is the nutritional value of your favorite breakfast cereal?  Do you know how many calories are in a one-ounce serving?  How could you find out?
- What uses, other than food, can you think of for eggs?  How might a manufacturer use eggs in his products?

_____

**Focus Question...**
- Eggs, as well as many other foods, contain protein, fat, minerals, and water.  What percentage of an average egg do you think is water?

_____

**Problem...**
Joy has been selling extra eggs from her chickens.  Yesterday, one of the buyers asked her how many cubic inches her eggs are.  What do you think would have been a reasonable answer for her to give?

**Cubic Inches**

| | |
|---|---|
| 1 | |
| 2 | |
| 3 | |
| 4 | |
| 5 | |
| 6 | |
| 7 | |
| 8 or more | |

# VOLUME OF AN EGG

## Objectives
- to select appropriate units and tools for measuring to the degree of accuracy required in a particular situation
- to extend students' understanding of the process of measurement
- to extend students' understanding of the concepts of volume, capacity, weight, and mass
- to model situations by carrying out experiments or simulations to determine probabilities

## Materials
A measuring cup, a pair of calipers, and an egg for each group of students

## Discussing
Divide the class into groups or have one group demonstrate. Give each group a measuring cup and an egg. What method(s) could they use to find the volume of the egg? What additional information might they need? (The number of cubic inches in a cup.) Ask students where they might find that information. (Many encyclopedias and dictionaries contain *Tables of Weights and Measures*, which will tell that one gallon contains 231 cubic inches.) How many cups are in a gallon? (Work this out as a group. There are 16 cups in a gallon.) Thus, the cubic inches in one full cup is $231\frac{1}{16}$, or 14.4.

## Graphing
Ask students to compare the length with the girth of their eggs. Does there seem to be a ratio? Can it be graphed? What type of graph might show this information?

## Mathing
One method is to break the egg, put the liquid into the measuring cup, then break the shell into small pieces which should sink into the liquid.

Can the volume of the egg be found without breaking the egg? Another method of finding volume would then be in order. If a larger measuring device is filled with one cup of water (or sand or dried beans) and the whole egg is placed inside, the water should rise to approximately $1\frac{1}{4}$ cup, showing that the displacement by the egg is $\frac{1}{4}$ cup. If so, the volume of the egg would then be $(\frac{1}{4}) \times 14.4$, or 3.6 cubic inches.

## Answering
The volume of most chicken eggs will be from 3 to 4 cubic inches.

## Extending
- Estimate the volume of other solid objects (onions, light bulbs, oranges, rocks...), then measure the volume using a measuring device.
- Estimate the volume of a potato, then try to justify your estimate by cutting the potato into cubic inches and lining up the blocks.

## BIRD SEED IN THE JAR

**Initial Graph...**
Has your family ever had a bird as a pet?  Mark your response on this graph.
Can you mark both areas?  Why or why not?

We have
never had
a pet bird.

We have
had a pet
bird.

**Speaking of Birds...**
- How many different kinds (species) of birds do you think live throughout the world?  How might these birds be grouped?  Is there any scientific way of classifying each bird?  Where might you find such information?
- How are birds important to humans?  In what ways do birds help humans?  In what ways might birds be harmful to humans?
- Do you think birds can talk to each other?  What kinds of messages do you think they might want or need to communicate?  Do birds communicate in any ways other than through songs or calls?
- If you wanted to study birds, what things would you be interested in finding out?  How might you go about finding information or getting help?

**Focus Question...**
- Have you ever heard anyone say, "So-and-so eats like a bird"?  What do birds eat?  Do they all eat the same things?  How much do birds eat in relation to their size?  What might happen to a human who really does "eat like a bird"?

**Problem...**
William must vary his bird's diet so that it eats one scoop of bird seed every day. He would like to store the seed in the large jar on the desk.  How many scoops of bird seed do you think it will take to fill the jar?

| | | |
|---|---|---|
| 1 _____ | 8 _____ | 15 _____ |
| 2 _____ | 9 _____ | 16 _____ |
| 3 _____ | 10 _____ | 17 _____ |
| 4 _____ | 11 _____ | 18 _____ |
| 5 _____ | 12 _____ | 19 _____ |
| 6 _____ | 13 _____ | 20 _____ |
| 7 _____ | 14 _____ | >20 _____ |

# BIRD SEED IN THE JAR

## Objectives
- to develop, analyze, and explain computation procedures and estimation techniques
- to develop, analyze, and explain methods for solving proportions
- to visualize and represent geometric figures with attention to developing spatial sense
- to understand the structure and use of systems of measurement

## Materials
A scoop, a jar, and some bird seed are necessary to complete this problem. (I generally use a coffee scoop or the measuring scoop from powdered diet food. I use a quart mayonnaise jar so I can take advantage of the rounded shape at the neck of the jar. I have the bird seed in a plastic bag. For **Reaching Out** you will need a bag of dried beans. You may also want to place a tray under the experiment to catch any seeds that may fall outside the jar.)

## Demonstrating
First, ask students to help you count as you fill the jar approximately one-third full. (You may want to shake the seeds down by lightly tapping the jar on the table.) Place a rubber band at that point and ask students if they would like to estimate again how many scoops fill the jar. Let a few students estimate this second time and ask them to explain why they did or did not choose a new number. Continue counting as you fill the jar just below the top curve in the jar. Shake the seeds down again. Ask students to estimate again. Some students will realize that the curvature at the top of the jar will make the last scoops fill up the jar at a faster linear rate. How many were correct in their original estimate?

## Graphing
Ask students to compare and graph the depth of the seeds in the jar with the number of scoops. Let them determine their own means of graphing, then discuss the various graphs and ask students to justify their selection.

## Answering
Using equipment I have, it takes 14 scoops to fill the jar. Results will vary depending upon the sizes of the scoop and jar.

## Extending
- Vary the diameter of the jars filled. How does the depth of the seed compare with the number of scoops as the jar's diameter increases? What if the jar's diameter decreases?
- William's mother bought some large dried beans on sale and wants to store them in jars the same size and shape as the jar that holds the bird seed. Since beans are much larger than bird seeds, William thinks it will take more scoops to fill the jar with beans. Or, is it less scoops? What does the class think and why?

  (Students should realize that a scoop is a scoop, no matter what is occupying that volume. Volume within the jar and within the scoop does not change. Therefore, results should not change.)

# PANS IN ORDER BY VOLUME

### Initial Graph...
How often do you help prepare a family meal at your house?  Make a mark that shows where your response would be along the graph below.

I have never
helped prepare
a family meal.

I help prepare
a family meal
every day.

### Problem...
Vivian found the six pans on the desk in her kitchen cupboard.  They all seem to hold a different volume and all are different shapes.  She has been trying to arrange them in order from the container with the smallest volume to the one with the largest volume.

She thinks that the smallest volume is in the container marked **D** and that the largest is in the container marked **A**.  Although she's not sure, she thinks the order is **D, F, B, C, E, A**.  Look at the pans and estimate what you think the order should be—from smallest to largest volume—and write it below Vivian's guess.

### Smallest to largest volume

D     F     B     C     E     A     (Vivian's guess)

# PANS IN ORDER BY VOLUME

## Objectives
- to understand the structure and use of systems of measurement
- to select appropriate units and tools for measuring to the degree of accuracy required in a particular situation
- to estimate, make, and use measurements to describe and compare phenomena
- to extend students' understanding of the concepts of perimeter, area, volume, capacity, and weight and mass

## Materials
You will need six different-sized and shaped containers, labeled A through F. (I use four cake pans and two casserole dishes and select a group that includes rectangular and circular pans of varying depths.)

## Discussing and Demonstrating
Begin by asking students to line up the containers in order from smallest to largest, then ask them to justify their choices.

Proof for the line-up of volume can be done by teacher or student demonstration. If the process is done by the teacher, ask students to tell you which steps should be done along the way. Students will soon notice that it is important to have a recorder in the group. Comparisons between containers can be done by filling each container in turn with a liquid or solid, such as water, sand, or rice, and measuring the volume of each into a known measuring device. At the conclusion, make a final check by pouring from one container to the next, beginning with the container of the largest volume. Each pouring should result in some of the liquid or solid remaining in the larger of the containers.

When the final arrangement has been determined, place the pans in order and ask students if they observe any factors in the shape of the pans that made them go in this order.

## Graphing
Ask students to construct a graph that would show the comparative volume of containers A–F. Asks them to verbalize the process, either as a whole-class discussion or within their small groups, before they begin the graph. Areas of consideration might include how to measure the volume, what information should be graphed, and the type of graph to be used.

## Mathing
Compare the measured volume of the shortest and tallest pans. What is their ratio? What is the difference in their heights? In their volumes? In their perimeters? Follow the same process with the longest and shortest pans and with the deepest and most shallow.

## Answering
The containers can be placed in order from the smallest volume to the largest volume by using the method described above.

## Extending
Could the problem have been solved using only the containers themselves as measuring devices? Try it with six different containers.

# VOLUME TO SURFACE AREA

### Initial Graph...
Someone has started a list identifying surfaces and what they cover. Can you add any items? Write your responses below.

| SKIN | is the surface of | A BODY |
|------|-------------------|--------|
| ICE | is the surface of | A FROZEN LAKE |
| | is the surface of | |
| | is the surface of | |
| | is the surface of | |

### Speaking of Surfaces...
- Which of the surfaces on the list completely surround the object?
- What is the geometric shape of each surface on the list? What is the average thickness of each surface? Is each the same thickness in all places? Arrange the above list in order from thinnest to thickest surface.
- What is the texture of each of the above surfaces? Is it smooth? Rough? Reflective? Colorless? Tough?

### Focus Question...
- How is surface area measured? Choose an object in this room, then describe and measure the surface area of that object.

### Problem...
Jake has arranged 36 blocks into the shape of a box (called a rectangular solid). Each block is one unit by one unit by one unit. He says that the total surface area of the box is 80 square units. Which of the following dimensions describe the measurements of the box Jake made?

1 x 3 x 12 _____

1 x 1 x 36 _____

1 x 2 x 18 _____

1 x 4 x 9 _____

2 x 3 x 6 _____

3 x 3 x 4 _____

2 x 2 x 9 _____

6 x 6 x 6 _____

# VOLUME TO SURFACE AREA

## Objectives
- to understand and apply geometric properties and relationships
- to represent and solve problems using geometric models
- to visualize and represent geometric figures with attention to developing spatial sense
- to extend students' understanding of the concepts of perimeter, area, and volume

## Discussing
Could any of the given dimensions be eliminated immediately because they were not made of the original 36 cubes? (The one rectangular solid with a volume other than 36 is the last one listed: 6 x 6 x 6. Students can verify this by multiplying all three dimensions.)

## Mathing
The next step is to verify the surface area. Ask a student to demonstrate the surface area of the first box (1 x 3 x 12) by diagram or construction, then determine each side's surface area.

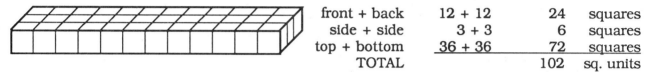

| | | | |
|---|---|---|---|
| front + back | 12 + 12 | 24 | squares |
| side + side | 3 + 3 | 6 | squares |
| top + bottom | 36 + 36 | 72 | squares |
| TOTAL | | 102 | sq. units |

Now, ask students to use the same method to verify their answer to the original problem.

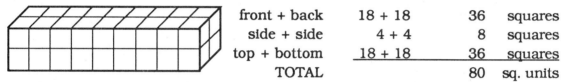

| | | | |
|---|---|---|---|
| front + back | 18 + 18 | 36 | squares |
| side + side | 4 + 4 | 8 | squares |
| top + bottom | 18 + 18 | 36 | squares |
| TOTAL | | 80 | sq. units |

The first example had a surface area of 102; the second 80. Do students notice a difference in basic shape? (The second figure is taller.) Ask them to guess which box has the largest surface area (1 x 1 x 36) and which has the smallest (3 x 3 x 4)?

## Graphing
The following chart lists all possible cube boxes with volume 36 and various surface areas.

| Dimensions | Surface Area | Dimensions | Surface Area |
|---|---|---|---|
| 1 x 1 x 36 | 146 | 1 x 6 x 6 | 96 |
| 1 x 2 x 18 | 112 | 2 x 2 x 9 | 80 |
| 1 x 3 x 12 | 102 | 2 x 3 x 6 | 72 |
| 1 x 4 x 9 | 98 | 3 x 3 x 4 | 66 |

## Answering
Dimensions of the box with a volume of 36 and a surface area of 80 are 2 x 2 x 9.

## Extending
How many different-shaped boxes can be made with 72 blocks? Find the surface area of each.

| Dimensions | Surface Area | Dimensions | Surface Area | Dimensions | Surface Area |
|---|---|---|---|---|---|
| 1 x 1 x 72 | 290 | 1 x 6 x 12 | 180 | 2 x 4 x 9 | 124 |
| 1 x 2 x 36 | 220 | 1 x 8 x 9 | 178 | 2 x 6 x 6 | 120 |
| 1 x 3 x 24 | 198 | 2 x 2 x 18 | 152 | 3 x 3 x 8 | 114 |
| 1 x 4 x 18 | 188 | 2 x 3 x 12 | 132 | 3 x 4 x 6 | 108 |

# BEST FRIEND IN SCIENCE

**Initial Graph...**
Mark your response to the question on the graph below.

### During science labs, I most enjoy working:

| alone | in pairs | in groups of 3 or 4 | in groups of 5 or more |
|-------|----------|---------------------|------------------------|
|       |          |                     |                        |

**Speaking of School...**
- Do you have classes in school where you work in teams? How are those teams chosen?
- What are the advantages of working or learning together in groups? What are the disadvantages?
- Do you enjoy learning in cooperative groups? How might you make a new person feel welcome in your group?

**Focus Question...**
- Do you have a certain friend that you generally try to work with on science projects? How many science labs have you had this year? How many times have you worked with your chosen partner? What percentage of the total science labs is that?

**Problem...**
Douglas and Philip are in a science class with 26 other students. The teacher is going to put them into groups of four for science lab. What are the chances that Douglas and Philip will be in the same science lab group?

### Chance (in %) that Douglas and Philip will work together

| 0–10% |  |
|-------|--|
| 11–20% |  |
| 21–30% |  |
| 31–40% |  |
| 41–50% |  |
| 51–60% |  |
| 61–70% |  |
| 71–80% |  |
| 81–90% |  |
| 91–100% |  |

# BEST FRIEND IN SCIENCE

## Objectives

- to model situations by experiments or simulations to determine probabilities
- to appreciate the power of using a probability model by comparing experimental results with mathematical expectations
- to make predictions that are based on experimental or theoretical probabilities
- to develop an appreciation for the pervasive use of probability in the real world

## Graphing

Suppose the other members of the science class are numbered 1-26 and Douglas and Philip are symbolized by **D** and **P**, respectively, then a lab team could consist of:

| 1,2,3,4 | 1,2,4,5 | 1,2,5,6 | 1,2,6,7 | ••• |
| 1,2,3,5 | 1,2,4,6 | 1,2,5,7 | 1,2,6,8 | ••• |
| 1,2,3,6 | 1,2,4,7 | 1,2,5,8 | 1,2,6,9 | ••• |
| ••• | ••• | ••• | ••• | ••• |

Continuing these combinations seems to "take forever." How about attacking a similar problem with fewer students? If there were only 4 students (1, 2, **D**, **P**), then there would be a 100% chance that the friends would be on the same team. With 8 students (1, 2, 3, 4, 5, 6, **D**, **P**), a listing of all possible combinations would be:

| 1234 | 1245 | 1256 | 126D | 12**DP** |
| 1235 | 1246 | 125D | 126P | |
| 1236 | 124D | 125P | | |
| 123D | 124P | | | |
| 123P | | | | |

(5 + 4 + 3 + 2 + 1) group of **15**

| 2345 | 2356 | 236D | 23**DP** |
| 2346 | 235D | 236P | |
| 234D | 235P | | |
| 234P | | | |

(4 + 3 + 2 + 1) group of **10**

| 3456 | 236D | 23**DP** |
| 345D | 236P | |
| 345P | | |

(3 + 2 + 1) group of **6**

| 456D | 45**DP** |
| 456P | |

(2 + 1) group of **3**          56**DP**} group of **1**

Notice that of the 15 possible combinations in the first group, only one has a Douglas-Philip pair. One of the 10 combinations in the next group has the desired pair. A pattern forms, giving a total of 5 out of 35 combinations (or 14%) where they will work together. At this point many students realize their answer for the original problem must be wrong. You may want to extend the problem to 12 students. However, an easier method might be found by analyzing the pattern from the 8 students.

## Discussing

Ask students how they justified the probability of the two friends being on the same team. Did they consider a list of all possibilities? Can they see any patterns developing?

## Answering

In a class of 28, one D-P pair would appear in each of the following groups: 1, 3, 6, 10, 15, 21, 28, 36, 45, 55, 66, 78, 91, 105, 120, 136, 153, 171, 190, 210, 231, 253, 276, 300, 325. This allows them to be on the same team 25 times out of 2925 possible combinations, or less than 1%.

## Extending

If the teacher groups the class of 28 students into four teams of seven each, what is the chance that Douglas and Philip will be on the same team?

# TOSSING A PENNY

**Initial Graph...**
When the team captains toss a coin at the beginning of a football game, what is the probability of the coin coming up heads?  Mark your response on the line graph below.

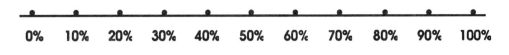

0%    10%    20%    30%    40%    50%    60%    70%    80%    90%    100%

**Speaking of Coin Tosses...**
- At what other times have you seen a coin tossed?  Have you ever heard someone say, "I'll toss you for it"?  Do you think that means that they are going to throw you around?  If not, why would they say that?

- In some countries coins are not circular.  What other shapes do coins have in other countries?  What shapes did coins have several hundred years ago?  How can you find out?  Do you think that the shape of the coin affects the probability of heads?

- Historically, how long have coins been in use?  What are coins made of?  How are they made?  Where are coins made in the United States?

**Focus Question...**
- How could you check the probability of heads for a tossed penny?  What objects could you toss, other than a coin, that would give the same probability?  How could you change a coin to give a different probability for heads?  What problems might this change create?

**Problem...**
Dino and Pietro each have a penny.  Dino has suggested that each toss his coin and, if they come up with a match (either both heads or both tails), then Pietro will cook dinner tonight.  If one coin comes up heads and the other tails, however, Dino will cook tonight.  Pietro isn't quite sure if this is fair.  Who do you think has a higher chance of cooking tonight's dinner?

| Pietro | |
|---|---|
| Dino | |
| Equal Chance | |

# TOSSING A PENNY

## Objectives

- to model situations by devising and carrying out experiments or simulations to determine probabilities
- to model situations by constructing a sample space to determine probabilities
- to appreciate the power of using a probability model by comparing experimental results with mathematical expectations
- to make predictions that are based on experimental or theoretical probabilities
- to develop an appreciation for the pervasive use of probability in the real world

## Materials

One penny for each student in the class

## Demonstrating and Discussing

Distribute pennies. Have students pair off and keep score under similar circumstances. One should get a point if the tossed coins match and the other a point if they do not. After a few minutes, ask the teams if it obvious who will win. If the teams combine results, does it then become obvious? Ask students to justify their answers to the problem.

## Graphing

Let **H** represent a head and **T** a tail. There are two coins, so $H_p$ represents the head on the Pietro's coin, $H_d$ the head on Dino's coin, and so on. The different possible arrangements may be listed in the following order.

$H_p$ — $H_d$ → Pietro will cook.

$H_p$ — $T_d$ → Dino will cook.

$T_p$ — $T_d$ → Pietro will cook.

$T_p$ — $H_d$ → Dino will cook.

Branching techniques can also be used to demonstrate the probability, with the concept of Dino tossing his coin first and Pietro next:

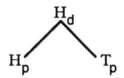 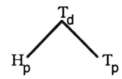

This is yet another way of demonstrating four arrangements with two matching and two not matching.

## Answering

Dino was playing fair, for each has two chances out of four (50%) of cooking dinner.

## Extending

Suppose another person joined Dino and Pietro in tossing coins. The rules for the coin toss have now changed in the following manner:

The third person has to cook tonight if all three coins are the same.

Pietro has to cook if there is only one head in the group.

Dino has to cook if there is only one tail in the group.

Now who has the highest chance of cooking dinner tonight? Who has the least chance? Graph the results.

# SPINNING SUMS

### Initial Graph...
Put a check mark on the spinner which would spin a 1 more frequently.

 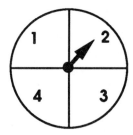

### Speaking of Spinners...
- What is the probability of spinning a 1 on the first spinner shown above? On the second spinner? What is the probability of spinning a 2 on each spinner? If you used both spinners, what would be your probability of getting a 3 on at least one of them?
- How is probability determined on a spinner? Does the probability change if the shape of the spinner is not circular? How might different shapes affect the probability? What if the shape was irregular (different sized sides)?

### Focus Question...
- What games do you play that use spinners? How are the spinners used in these games? Invent a game that would use the two spinners above. What are the rules?

### Problem...
Yung and Kaitlan each have one of the spinners shown at the top of this page. They will each spin their own spinner then add the two results and record the final sum. For example, if they should spin as shown above (1 and 2), a sum of 3 would be recorded. If they do this several times, which of the following sums do you think will come up most frequently? Circle the numeral that shows your choice.

**Sum:**    0    1    2    3    4    5    6    7    8

# SPINNING SUMS

## Objectives
- to model situations by devising and carrying out experiments or simulations to determine probabilities
- to model situations by constructing a sample space to determine probabilities
- to appreciate the power of using a probability model by comparing experimental results with mathematical expectations
- to make predictions that are based on experimental or theoretical probabilities
- to develop an appreciation for the pervasive use of probability in the real world

## Materials
Spinners can be easy and fun to make out of paper clips (one for a stem at the center and another for a spinning hand) and notecards. It is easier to divide the face of the card into three or four parts and number them before the stem is placed through the center. The stem can be formed by bending one end of a paper clip at 90° to its body. The body of the stem can be taped down on the underside of the card after the stem itself is pierced through the face of the card. The other paper clip is used as the hand of the spinner and should be placed loosely over the stem.

## Graphing
After students make spinners, they can observe results as they record sums from a spinner of three sections and another of four sections. As they record the sums many times, a definite pattern will appear. Combine the results to emphasize the pattern.

Another approach might be to use the branching technique where one spinner result is considered first and lines branch out to results of the second spinner. (See page 148.)

## Mathing
Results may be justified by listing all possible combinations from the two spinners and their sums:

| spinner with 3 sections | 1 | 2 | 3 | 1 | 2 | 3 | 1 | 2 | 3 | 1 | 2 | 3 |
|---|---|---|---|---|---|---|---|---|---|---|---|---|
| spinner with 4 sections | 1 | 1 | 1 | 2 | 2 | 2 | 3 | 3 | 3 | 4 | 4 | 4 |
| SUMS | 2 | 3 | 4 | 3 | 4 | 5 | 4 | 5 | 6 | 5 | 6 | 7 |

Of the 12 possible combinations, one is a **sum 2**, two are a **sum 3**, etc. Hence the chance of **sum 2** is 1 out of 12, of **sum 3** is 2 out of 12, etc. Notice that the probability for **sum 2** and **sum 7** is identical, as are the probability for **sum 3** and **sum 6** and for **sum 4** and **sum 5**.

## Answering
Sums 4 and 5 have equal and highest frequency for the spinners in this problem.

## Extending
What if the sections on each spinner were not all equal? What if, as shown below, one spinner had one-third of its area labeled 1 and two-thirds labeled 2, and the other spinner had one-fourth of its area labeled 1, two-fourths labeled 2, and one-fourth labeled 3?

   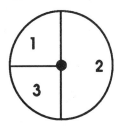

How would the chance of specific sums be affected? Which sums would appear with the greatest frequency?

# LINE UP THE CARDS

### Initial Graph...
If you had two cards, one with an 'H' and one with an 'I,' what chance would you have of putting them down in random order and having them form the word 'Hi'? Mark your response on the line below.

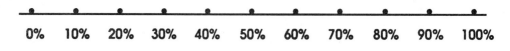

0%   10%   20%   30%   40%   50%   60%   70%   80%   90%   100%

### Speaking of Probability...
- On what basis did you determine your probability? Did you make a model and try the activity several times?
- How many different words, including nonsense words, can be formed using these two cards?

### Focus Question...
- If you could add one more lettered card to the 'H' and the 'I,' what letter would you choose? Now how many different words would be possible? How does the probability of a specific word change?

### Problem...
Cornelius has four cards: one with a letter B, one with a letter I, one with a letter R, and one with a letter D. He wants to use them to spell the word "Bird."

He shuffles the cards, then turns them face down, one at a time, on the table in front of him, placing them left to right. What is the chance that any two of the letters will be in the correct spot (B first, I second, R third, and D fourth) when he turns the cards face up?

# LINE UP THE CARDS

## Objectives

- to model situations through experiments or simulations to determine probabilities
- to model situations by constructing a sample space to determine probabilities
- to appreciate the power of using a probability model by comparing experimental results with mathematical expectations
- to make predictions that are based on experimental or theoretical probabilities
- to develop an appreciation for the pervasive use of probability in the real world

## Materials

Four cards for each student or group of students (The cards should be the same on one side to eliminate cheating. If you wish, you can use playing cards and any defined order for placement upon the table.)

## Graphing

In this problem it is more convenient to record the possibilities of all four cards and note the following information, making tallies to the right for each attempt.

| | |
|---|---|
| 0 cards in place | |
| 1 card in place | |
| 2 cards in place | |
| 3 cards in place | |
| all cards in place | |

Now probability can be found for all five cases. It helps to expand the probability by combining class results.

Justification can be found by listing all arrangements of the letters B, I, R, D where order indicates arrangement upon the table (the number of cards **in place** is in parenthesis):

| | | | | | |
|---|---|---|---|---|---|
| **BIRD** (4) | **BI**DR (2) | **B**DIR (1) | **B**DR**I** (2) | **B**RI**D** (2) | **B**RDI (1) |
| I**BRD** (2) | IBDR (0) | IR**BD** (1) | IRDB (0) | IDBR (0) | IDRB (1) |
| R**BI**D (1) | RBDI (0) | R**IB**D (2) | R**I**DB (1) | RDBI (0) | RDIB (0) |
| DBIR (0) | DB**RI** (1) | DIBR (1) | DI**R**B (2) | DRBI (0) | DRIB (0) |

## Mathing

Thus, the chance of having no cards in place is 9/24, of having only one card in place is 8/24, of having two cards in place is 6/24, of having three cards in place is 0, and of having all four cards in place is 1/24.

## Answering

There is a 33% chance (or 6/24, or 1 out of 3) that two cards will be in the correct location.

## Extending

- How would the probability change if there were a card for each letter of the name Michael? Following the same procedure, what is the chance that any two of the letters would be in the correct spot?

- The first three places on a car license plate are letters. If all letters of the alphabet were used on license plates, what is the probability that the letters would form the word "HIP"?

# TWO PURPLES IN A ROW

**Initial Graph...**
If you had a sack of purple, white, red, green, yellow, and blue marbles, which would be your favorite color? Mark your response below.

| Purple | White | Red | Green | Yellow | Blue |
|--------|-------|-----|-------|--------|------|

**Speaking of Marbles...**
- Do you have any marbles? Are they solid colors or "marbled"? Are they all the same size? What do you use them for?
- Where can you buy marbles? Can you buy them one at a time or do they come only in packages? How many are in a package and about what does a package cost? How much would this be per marble?
- When was the first marble made? Where do they make marbles today, and how are they made? What type of material are they made of?

**Focus Question...**
- If you had one purple marble and one white marble in a sack, what would be the probability of drawing out a purple marble?
- What if the sack contained two purple and two white marbles? Then what would be the probability of drawing a purple marble?

**Problem...**
Pilár had two purple and two white marbles in a sack. If she takes out one marble at a time, what is the probability that she will draw two purple marbles in a row? Mark the range on the graph that includes your choice.

| 0 – 20% | 21 – 40% | 41 – 60% | 61 – 80% | 81 – 100% |
|---------|----------|----------|----------|-----------|

# TWO PURPLES IN A ROW

## Objectives
- to model situations by devising and carrying out experiments or simulations to determine probabilities
- to model situations by constructing a sample space to determine probabilities
- to appreciate the power of using a probability model by comparing experimental results with mathematical expectations
- to make predictions that are based on experimental or theoretical probabilities
- to develop an appreciation for the pervasive use of probability in the real world

## Materials
Several bags of marbles, each containing 2 pair of different colors (colored poker chips, tokens, or cubes will work well)

## Demonstrating
Ask students to shake the bags then draw out the four items, one at a time, and record the results. Working in pairs is time efficient, as one student can shake the bag and draw the marbles while the other records the results. After about 25 draws per student, combine the recorded data for a class graph.

## Graphing
Ask the students to justify the probability of drawing two consecutive items of the same color. One method might be to list, in order from right to left, all possible ways the four marbles in the problem might be drawn (P = purple, W = white, so PWWP represents drawing a purple first, a white second and third, and a purple last).

    **PP**WW       PWPW       PWWP       W**PP**W       WPWP       WW**PP**

Notice that three of the six arrangements have two consecutive purples (**PP**).

Branching is yet another method to demonstrate the drawings with the first drawing on the top line, second on second, and so on:

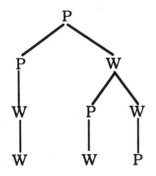 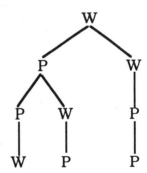

Again, there are 6 possible arrangements with 3 indicating two consecutively-drawn purple marbles.

## Answering
There is a 50% (or 3/6 or 1/2) chance of drawing two purple marbles in a row.

## Extending
- Out of a sack of **ten** marbles—two white, four red, and four purple—what is the probability of drawing two purple marbles in a row?
- Given the original contents of the sack (2 purple and 2 white marbles), suppose the drawn marble is replaced after each draw, so that each draw is from a sack with two purples and two whites. If there are four draws, what is the probability that two purple marbles will be drawn in a row?

# EITHER-OR...NEITHER-NOR

## Initial Graph...
What color hair do you have? Mark your response on the graph below.

| Blonde | Red | Brown | Black | White | Mixed |
|--------|-----|-------|-------|-------|-------|
|        |     |       |       |       |       |

## Speaking of Hair Color...
- What is the probability of being a blond in this class? What about the other hair colors—what is the probability of each?
- How many people in this class have either blond or red hair? From the class graph, what is the probability of someone in this class having **either** blond **or** red hair?
- How many people in this class have **neither** brown **nor** white hair? What is the probability of someone in the class having some hair color other than brown or white?

## Focus Question...
- What do the words "either-or" and "neither-nor" mean to you? Use each word pair in a sentence.

## Problem...
Hamil has a sack of marbles. Two of the marbles are white, five are blue, eight are orange, and ten are purple. He will shake the bag and draw only one marble. What is the probability that the marble he draws will fall into the following categories? Mark your response to each category on the graph.

| Either purple or white | Neither orange nor blue |
|------------------------|-------------------------|
|                        |                         |

 © 1990 Midwest Publications • Critical Thinking Press & Software, P.O. Box 448, Pacific Grove, CA  93950

# EITHER-OR...NEITHER-NOR

## Objectives

- to model situations by devising and carrying out simulations to determine probabilities
- to model situations by constructing a sample space to determine probabilities
- to compare experimental results with mathematical expectations
- to make predictions that are based on experimental or theoretical probabilities
- to develop an appreciation for the pervasive use of probability in the real world
- to systematically collect, organize, and describe data

## Materials

Several sacks of marbles or tokens, each with the same numbers and colors as the problem

## Graphing

Several groups could draw, with each group having a recorder. Since the total number of draws is important, they should either be marked by color to the side or kept in tally form:

| Marbles Drawn | Either Purple or White | Neither Orange nor Blue |
|---|---|---|
| ̶T̶H̶L̶  ̶T̶H̶L̶  I | ̶T̶H̶L̶ | ̶T̶H̶L̶  I |

Ask three students, one for each category, to tally the combined results. Combining results from the different groups into a class graph will expand the chance of close results.

## Mathing

The first thing most students say while trying to justify results is that out of the 25 total marbles, ten are purple hence the probability of drawing a purple marble is $^{10}/_{25}$. With similar logic, the probability of an orange marble is $^8/_{25}$, a blue marble $^5/_{25}$, and a white marble $^2/_{25}$. Letting **P** represent purple, etc., the first draw could be any of the following.

**P P P P P P P P P P O O O O O O O O B B B B B W W**

This entire list could then be rearranged in two ways:

| Either Purple or White |
|---|
| **P P P P P P P P P P W W** |

**O O O O O O O O B B B B B**

*or*

| Neither Orange nor Blue |
|---|
| **P P P P P P P P P P W W** |

**O O O O O O O O B B B B B**

## Discussing

Some students are shocked when they first realize that **either purple or white** is the same group as **neither orange nor blue.** When would that not be the case? Both groups above show that the probability desired is $^{12}/_{25}$. Did anyone approach this problem differently?

Notice again the probability of each color. If we symbolize the probability of purple by Pr(P), orange by Pr(O), blue by Pr(B), and white by Pr(W), then:

$$Pr(P) = \frac{10}{25} \qquad Pr(O) = \frac{8}{25} \qquad Pr(B) = \frac{5}{25} \qquad Pr(W) = \frac{2}{25}$$

Notice that $Pr(\text{either P or W}) = Pr(P) + Pr(W) = \frac{10}{25} + \frac{2}{25} = \frac{12}{25}$;

and that $Pr(\text{neither O nor B}) = Pr(\text{marbles}) - Pr(O) - Pr(B) = \frac{25}{25} - \frac{8}{25} - \frac{5}{25} = \frac{12}{25}$.

## Answering

The probability that the marble drawn will fit either category is 48%, or $^{12}/_{25}$.

## Extending

Given the same sack of marbles, what would be the probability that, of the first **two** marbles drawn, both are either purple or white?

# COMPARISON OF HOLIDAYS

**Problem...**

Maggie loves holidays. She likes Thanksgiving, with the family gatherings and turkey and pumpkin pie. She likes Halloween, with the fun of dressing up and getting treats. She likes April Fool's Day and waits all year to pull surprise tricks on her friends.

Help Maggie find out which of these is the most popular holiday by marking an **X** in the column of your choice.

| THANKSGIVING | HALLOWEEN | APRIL FOOL'S |
|---|---|---|
|  |  |  |

# COMPARISON OF HOLIDAYS

## Objectives
- to systematically collect, organize, and describe data
- to construct, read, and interpret tables, charts, and graphs
- to make inferences and convincing arguments that are based on data analysis
- to evaluate arguments that are based on data analysis
- to develop an appreciation for statistical methods as a means for decision making

## Graphing
Generally, the first method mentioned is to total the number of Xs for each holiday and give the results numerically. This can be done directly on the graph while you circle Xs in groups of ten to emphasize place value. The numerical score can be placed at the end of each column.

There are many other ways of displaying the results. Some students may not like numerical results. (Ask them why they feel a need for a different form. Perhaps it is difficult for them to see the difference between the three choices with numbers.) A bar graph is frequently a second choice. Others may suggest a line graph, a pictograph, or a circle graph.

| | |
|---|---|
| Thanksgiving— 10 | Thanksgiving 👤👤👤👤👤👤👤👤👤👤 |
| Halloween— 14 | Halloween 👤👤👤👤👤👤👤👤👤👤👤👤👤👤 |
| April Fool's Day— 4 | April Fool's Day 👤👤👤👤 |

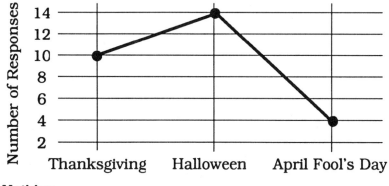

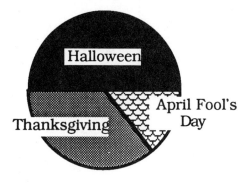

## Mathing
Ask students to compare the responses recorded on the bar, circle, and line graphs. Can they use any of the graphs to find percentage?

## Discussing
The circle graph may be hardest to display. Talk about the steps of dividing a circle into parts. In the above case, with 28 responses the circle needed to be divided into 28 equal parts. A large circle could be drawn on the board and divided into two equal parts (14 on each side), then into fourths (7 in each section) and the last part done by estimation. A more accurate method would be to calculate the number of degrees (360 ÷ 28) for each participant. Ask students to identify other possible display methods (pictorial,... ). Of the methods discussed, which appears to display the results best?

## Answering
Use different graphs (numerical, bar, line, pictorial, circle) to record the poll results.

## Extending
Ask students to name five professional or local sports teams, then have them help identify a class favorite by placing an X under the team of their choice. Display results in a graph.

# GRAPHING A FAVORITE BEVERAGE

**Problem...**

Terry and Charlotte want to have a party for 100 of their friends. Some of their friends like grape drink, others orange juice, and so on. They need help deciding how much of each beverage to order.

If you were to go to their party, which beverage would you like to drink? For each full can that you might drink during a three-hour party, place an **X** after your choice. You may choose more than one, and it is permissible to pick different beverages (i.e., 2 grape drinks and 1 cream soda).

Cola _____

Orange Juice _____

Orange Soda _____

Fruit Punch _____

Grape Drink _____

Cream Soda _____

Lemon-Lime Soda _____

Lemonade _____

Iced Tea _____

Root Beer _____

# GRAPHING A FAVORITE BEVERAGE

## Objectives
- to systematically collect, organize, and describe data
- to construct, read, and interpret tables, charts, and graphs
- to make inferences and convincing arguments that are based on data analysis
- to evaluate arguments that are based on data analysis
- to develop an appreciation for statistical methods as a means for decision making

## Graphing
Ask students to record the statistical results in various ways (numeric, bar, line, pictorial, or circle graphs). You may want to divide the class into groups and ask each group to display their results using one or more of the methods. Ask the groups to collect and record all their results on a class graph on the chalkboard.

## Discussing
On the basis of the class results, what is the favorite beverage? How many beverages does the average student drink (divide total beverages by total number of students)? How could one calculate how many of each beverages to order for the party?

## Mathing
As an example, assume that students in one class say they would consume the following beverages during a three-hour party.

| | | | |
|---|---|---|---|
| Cola | 14 | Orange Juice | 0 |
| Orange Soda | 1 | Fruit Punch | 6 |
| Grape Drink | 18 | Cream Soda | 4 |
| Lemon-Lime Soda | 8 | Lemonade | 0 |
| Iced Tea | 0 | Root Beer | 9 |

| | |
|---|---|
| Total number of students | 22 |
| Total number of beverages | 60 |

According to this sample, the average student drinks $^{60}/_{22}$, or 2.73 beverages. If Terry and Charlotte's other 78 friends were similar to the sample, they would need $100 \times 2.73$, or 273 cans of beverages for the party. For each choice, the total number of cans would be:

Cola: $\frac{14}{60} \times 273 = 64$          Orange Soda: $\frac{1}{60} \times 273 = 5$

Fruit Punch: $\frac{6}{60} \times 273 = 27$          Grape Drink: $\frac{18}{60} \times 273 = 82$

Cream Soda: $\frac{4}{60} \times 273 = 18$          Lemon-Lime Soda: $\frac{8}{60} \times 273 = 36$

Root Beer: $\frac{9}{60} \times 273 = 41$

## Answering
The final number of each type of beverages needed for the 100 invited guests would be calculated as shown.

## Extending
- Repeat the activity using typical party snacks rather than beverages.
- Use the results from these two activities and grocery advertisements from a local newspaper to determine how much the food and beverages for the party would cost.

# TO THE NURSE

**Problem...**

Kareem has been to see the school nurse twice this week. He noticed that on one of the days he was there, few people were waiting to see the nurse. On the other day, however, several students were in the waiting room. Kareem started to wonder which day of the week the school nurse sees the most students.

Help him make a prediction by marking an **X** under each day of the week that you have seen the school nurse during the past two weeks. If you have not been to the nurse during the past two weeks, put your **X** in the last column.

| MON | TUE | WED | THURS | FRI | NO NURSE CARE |
|-----|-----|-----|-------|-----|---------------|
|     |     |     |       |     |               |

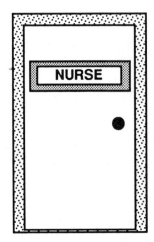

# TO THE NURSE

## Objectives
- to systematically collect, organize, and describe data
- to construct, read, and interpret tables, charts, and graphs
- to make inferences and convincing arguments that are based on data analysis
- to evaluate arguments that are based on data analysis
- to develop an appreciation for statistical methods as a powerful means for decision making

## Graphing
Ask students to determine from their information if there is one day of the week that students visit the nurse more than the other days of the week. (You might verify the information by asking your school nurse or by asking students to keep records for a week or two prior to using this problem.) When students have agreed on the day of the week that has the greatest number of students in the nurse's office, they have determined the **mode**. Ask students to explain how the mode might be visually verified by observing different methods of displaying these statistics?

- In a numeric graph the mode would be the day of the week with the largest value.
- In a line or bar graph the mode would be the tallest or longest point or bar.
- In a circle graph the mode would be the largest "piece of the pie."

## Mathing
Ask students to use the statistics gathered to find the average number of visits for each day of the week. Can they compare the **mean** (see page 167), the **median** (see page 169), and the **mode**?

## Discussing
Help students determine real-life applications for the gathered data. *"In what ways would knowing the information gathered in this problem help the school nurse? Would it be valuable to anyone else in the school? If so, who and why? What other businesses might use 'frequency of use' data for planning?"*

## Answering
At our school, Friday is the **mode**—the day of the week with most visits to the nurse. However, schools vary due to programs offered or availability of nurse care.

## Extending
Use various topics and time-diaries to gather information and graph it using different methods. Find the mode for each set of statistics. Topics might include:

- hours of television watched each day of the week.
- hours spent per day doing ... (reading, sports, homework, chores).
- grade on last spelling (or any other subject) test.

# BIRTHDAY MONTH

**Problem...**
Beth Ann was born January 24, 1977, so her birth month is JANUARY. She hopes that at least one of you will share her birthday month. Help her determine the birthday months for your classmates by placing an **X** after the correct month for each member of the class.

January _____

February _____

March _____

April _____

May _____

June _____

July _____

August _____

September _____

October _____

November _____

December _____

# BIRTHDAY MONTH

## Objectives
- to systematically collect, organize, and describe data
- to construct, read, and interpret tables, charts, and graphs
- to make inferences and convincing arguments that are based on data analysis
- to evaluate arguments that are based on data analysis
- to develop an appreciation for statistical methods as a powerful means for decision making

## Graphing
This problem again emphasizes the **mode** of gathered statistics. List the most frequent month(s) and write the label **mode**. It is possible to have more than one mode for a graph.

## Discussing
Ask students questions to help them analyze the data on the graph. *"How many students in this class share Beth Ann's birth month? Do any months have more responses? Within this classroom, which month or months have the greatest number of birthdays?"*

## Answering
The mode for birth months for your class can be found from the highest resulting tally beside each month.

## Extending
- Compare the mode for the class with that of the school. In several schools it is relatively easy to obtain a list of birth dates.
- Extend the information on class birthdays to a two-dimensional graph (month and day of the month) like the one shown below.

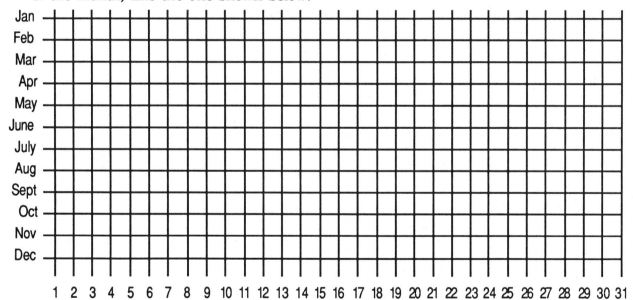

- Find the mode of both the birth month and the birth day. Would the results be the same if the entire grade-level were included? The school? Families? This might make an interesting long-term project for a group of students or a class.

# BEATS PER MINUTE

Lucia and Suhali each timed their heart rate during health class. Suhali who had been sitting quietly reading a book, said that his heart was beating 70 times a minute. Lucia, who had been late for class and had just run down the hallway, said that her heart was beating 120 times a minute. The teacher said that the **average** of their heart rates was 95 beats per minute.

_____

### Problem...
- Sit quietly for 1 minute, then find your pulse and count the number of times your heart beats in one minute. Write this number in the first box below.
- Stand beside your desk and run in place for 1 minute. Again, find your pulse and count the number of times your heart beats for the next **six seconds**. Multiply that number by 10. Write this product in the second box below.
- Find the average number of heartbeats for the two minutes you timed. Mark this average on the graph.

## Measured rates:

☐ **Heart rate after quiet**          ☐ **Heart rate after exercise**

## Average rate:

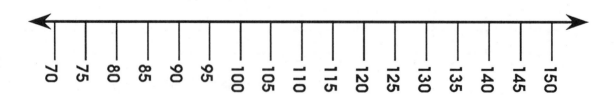

70  75  80  85  90  95  100  105  110  115  120  125  130  135  140  145  150

# BEATS PER MINUTE

**Objectives**
- to systematically collect, organize, and describe data
- to construct, read, and interpret tables, charts, and graphs
- to make inferences and convincing arguments that are based on data analysis
- to evaluate arguments that are based on data analysis
- to develop an appreciation for statistical methods as a powerful means for decision making

**Mathing**
One common method of figuring the arithmetic average of two numbers is to add the rates and divide by two.

$$\frac{70 + 120}{2} = \frac{190}{2} = 95.$$

**Graphing**
Another method is to consider the two numbers on the number line and find the number in the middle of the segment joining them.)

For instance, if the rates were 70 and 120 per minute, as measured in the problem example, the mean or arithmetic average would be:

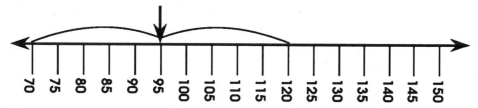

The distance from 70 to 95 = 25, and the distance from 120 to 95 = 25.

**Discussing**
Ask a pair of students to demonstrate how they arrived at their average, called the **mean**. Notice that if Lucia and Suhali combined their heart rates for one minute, they would have 70 + 120, or 190 beats. If someone's heart beat at exactly their average of 95 beats per minute and continued that for two minutes, they would also have 190 beats (2 × 160).

**Answering**
The average heart beats about 70 times per minute at rest and may reach twice that during or following periods of exercise.

**Extending**
- Find the average (mean) for the entire class.
- Determine a formula so that the mean of any number of rates can be determined. ($s_1 + s_2 + s_3 + \cdots + s_n + n$ = mean, when $s$ = individual rates and $n$ = number of individuals).

# SPOKEN WORDS PER MINUTE

Georgia and Angus were arguing about how many words each of them speaks per minute.  To reach an agreement, Georgia  talked about school for one minute while Angus made a tally mark for every ten words she said.  She's a fast talker, and the 23 tallies meant she had spoken 230 words per minute.

Then Angus talked for one minute about how to ride on a skate board, and Georgia  made a tally mark for every ten words he said.  He was easy to record, as he spoke clearly and slowly.  Georgia made 9 tally marks to represent the 90 words he had spoken.  They each numerically recorded their words per minute below.

**Problem...**
With a partner, find the number of words per minute you speak (not read aloud) at a normal pace.  Record the results below.

| Name | Words spoken per minute |
| --- | --- |
| Georgia | 230 |
| Angus | 90 |
|  |  |
|  |  |
|  |  |
|  |  |
|  |  |
|  |  |
|  |  |
|  |  |
|  |  |
|  |  |
|  |  |
|  |  |
|  |  |
|  |  |
|  |  |
|  |  |
|  |  |
|  |  |
|  |  |
|  |  |

 © 1990 Midwest Publications • Critical Thinking Press & Software, P.O. Box 448, Pacific Grove, CA  93950